The Economic Analysis of Trade Unions

The Economic Analysis of Trade Unions

Charles Mulvey

ST. MARTIN'S PRESS
New York

All rights reserved. For information, write:
St. Martin's Press, Inc., 175 Fifth Avenue, New York, N.Y. 10010

Printed in Great Britain
ISBN 0-312-22684-5

First Published in the United States of America in 1978

Library of Congress Cataloging in Publication Data

Mulvey, Charles.
The economic analysis of trade unions

Bibliography: p.
Includes indexes.
1. Trade-unions.   2. Labor economics.
I. Title.
HD6483.M78   331.88   78-9094

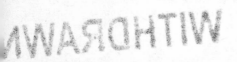

Contents

Preface

This book was written in the course of developing an empirically oriented research project which is being undertaken at Glasgow University. We set out to try to quantify the economic impact of trade union activity and as the project proceeded it became increasingly clear that the theoretical underpinnings of the economics of trade unions were nowhere set out clearly and comprehensively. Existing texts appeared to be dated or too narrow in their outlook and the journal literature is diffuse and usually technically advanced.

As I became increasingly familiar with the theoretical framework within which the research project was being developed, it seemed sensible to attempt to structure the elements of the analysis into textbook form. Hence this is intended as an elementary textbook on the economic aspects of trade unions. My aim has been to write a book accessible to students with only an elementary acquaintance with economic theory and no prior knowledge of industrial relations. So the only prerequisite for an understanding of the subject matter is a general understanding of the principles of consumer theory and 'supply and demand'. At the same time I have tried to make the book sufficiently comprehensive and suggestive of more complex matters as to be worthwhile reading for more advanced students of both labour economics and industrial relations. There are many topics touched on in the course of this book which are not developed within it, and the reader must be prepared to consult texts in both labour economics and industrial relations in order to gain a full understanding of the subject.

I have deliberately refrained from using mathematics as an expositional device; I have reported empirical results but have not (with one or two small exceptions) referred to econometric techniques: and, finally, I have everywhere tried to present a balanced and objective account of the subject and to suppress my personal prejudices. However, in chapter 11, I have expressed some personal views on economic policy which will no doubt prove controversial. The student may disagree with these views and in so doing will probably find himself engaged in a worthwhile and relevant exercise.

The theoretical sections owe much to the work of Cartter (1959) but attempt to go rather further, albeit in less detail, than he did. The empirical work which is reported in the second half of the book draws heavily on the project being carried out at Glasgow University.

It remains only to acknowledge those who have collaborated with me at Glasgow University in the research project which led me to write the book and those who helped me to clarify my approach to the subject – Professors L. C. Hunter and Albert Rees and my colleagues at Princeton University. My thanks are also due to Pauline Connelly for typing the manuscript with such efficiency. The research project is funded by the SSRC and is being conducted with the generous co-operation of the Department of Employment.

University of Glasgow and Princeton University · *Charles Mulvey*

CHAPTER 1

Introduction

The study of industrial relations has largely been divorced from the study of labour economics. There are many reasons for this situation, which is regretted by many but welcomed by others. It is nonetheless a fact that while much of the subject matter of the two disciplines is common to both, economists have examined the labour market mostly on the basis of the traditional apparatus of economic analysis whereas specialists in industrial relations have employed a multi-disciplinary approach which involves sociology, law, psychology and organisational theory.

The most pervasive institution in the labour market of most industrial countries is the trade union movement. The government, structure and organisation of trade unions are central to the industrial relations or 'institutional' approach to the study of the labour market. As a result the institutional character of trade union activity is the subject of a well developed body of analysis but one which is largely void of rigorous economic content. In contrast, economists have often apparently decided that trade unions are awkward animals to incorporate into their analytical models because they behave in 'irrational' ways, tend to pursue disequilibrating objectives and function to stifle the free operation of markets. Hence economists have generally either ignored trade unions altogether or attempted to characterise them by analogy with monopolistic firms. Those who have gone beyond such simplification have tended to do so in forays into particular aspects of union activity such as the economics of strikes or models of collective bargaining. A good deal of empirical work on the effects of trade unions has also been undertaken.

There are a number of exceptions to these generalisations. Certain economists have been concerned to develop an economic analysis of trade unions, most notably J. T. Dunlop (1950), Albert Rees (1962) and Alan Cartter (1959). In this book we do not intend to carry these analyses further in substance than the original authors. Our purpose is instead to develop a comprehensive economic analysis of trade unions which capitalises on these existing studies, to extend it to incorporate more recent developments in both the theoretical and empirical literature and to present the material in a systematic analytical framework such as exists for other economic phenomena.

To approach the subject of trade unions in this manner leaves us open to the charge that we are contributing further to the fragmentation of the study of

1

labour. It is a charge to which we must plead guilty. There are however, in our view, mitigating circumstances. Trade unions are multi-dimensional institutions of great complexity, and a comprehensive and integrated analysis of the many sides of their activity would be an ambitious task in the extreme. Arthur Ross (1948) probably came closest to attempting it but ended up by focusing on the very ambivalence of his subject. No doubt some brave spirit will rise to the challenge of attempting a comprehensive analysis of trade unions but we shall be less ambitious here.

Generations of students of labour have had to put up with the fact that labour market behaviour is taught, researched and written about from distinct economic and institutional standpoints. By and large they have also been required to synthesise these different approaches by themselves. It seems unlikely that this situation will alter significantly in the near future and this provides a rationale for our approach. First, we explicitly accept the dichotomy between the institutional and economic approaches to the labour market. Second, we go further and identify the role of the main institution in the labour market and single it out for special treatment. Hence we largely ignore the institutional aspects of the industrial relations system in which the trade union is a major participant, and we also neglect many of the aspects of labour market behaviour which occur independently of trade unions. Our justification is that the economic analysis of trade unions is a dimension of trade union activity which bears analysis in its own right, so that the student of labour may understand the economic dimensions of industrial relations and the economic implications of the behaviour of the trade union as an institution in the labour market.

The delimitation of the subject matter of this book is a conscious and explicit one and its implications are referred to where they seem relevant. Hence, where a topic is patently only comprehensible in the wider context of an industrial relations or labour market analysis, some indication of the further implications is given, with references to other work when appropriate.

The book is organised into two general parts. In the first half, chapters 2 to 7, an attempt is made to recognise the institutional character of trade unions and to present a coherent theoretical framework within which they may be analysed; in the second half, chapters 8 to 12, the main objective is to give some impression of the economic magnitudes associated with trade union activity and their implications for the economy and economic policy.

CHAPTER 2

The Institutional Setting

Since most of the remainder of this book is concerned only with the economics of trade unions this chapter is devoted to a brief and general consideration of trade unions as institutions. What we wish to describe here is the nature of trade unions as social, political and economic institutions and the process by which they developed. We can only make a gesture towards doing this, but it is necessary to grasp the great complexity of trade unionism if an economic analysis of trade union behaviour is to make any kind of sense.

Trade union growth — a general view

Trade union growth and development has been characterised historically by more or less distinctive *phases* of growth. These phases of growth have tended to occur as a response to economic, social, political or legal phenomena or combinations of them all. The first phase typically has been the formation of a number of small and localised trade unions confined to craftsmen. The second phase has generally involved the creation of non-craft unions which embraced the unskilled and which existed side by side with the craft unions. The third phase of growth has been the absorption of the semi-skilled or operative grades of labour from the mass-production industries into either the existing craft or non-craft unions, or into industrial unions representing all the workers in a particular industry. The fourth phase of growth has involved the organisation of white-collar workers into existing unions or into separate white-collar unions.

Now not all countries have experienced each of the phases of growth listed above. In some countries certain phases of growth have never occurred as distinctive phenomena while in others one or more phases of growth have occurred simultaneously. Moreover, within the context of the four phases of growth there have been important structural changes within the trade union movement which have served to blur the distinctions between one phase and another as a result of the consolidation of trade unions of different types into new or hybrid forms. Hence the 'phases of growth' identified above should be viewed only as a general descriptive characterisation of a complex and diverse process.

In the nineteenth century trade unionism was almost entirely confined to

3

craftsmen, although in Britain unions of unskilled workers had emerged in the last decade of the century. Hence at the beginning of the twentieth century the trade union movement comprised mainly craftsmen and was therefore insignificant in relation to the total labour force which could have been in trade unions. Table 2.1 below illustrates the pattern of trade union growth from 1900 to 1970 in four countries.

It may be readily observed from Table 2.1 that in 1900 the extent of unionism was relatively small in both the UK and the USA and the figures for the percentage unionised may be taken to refer mainly to craftsmen. The first phase of growth may therefore be approximately dated as continuing until around the turn of the century in Britain, the USA and Australia but lasting until somewhat later in Sweden. In the years leading up to the First World War the second phase of growth — the recruitment of unskilled workers into unions — occurred in varying degrees in the UK, the USA and Australia, but in Sweden did not begin until after the outbreak of war.

The timing of the third phase of growth is less easily distilled from a simple examination of the figures in the table. The severity of the economic depressions of the 1920s and 1930s took its toll of the established trade unions and it was not until the Second World War and the years immediately preceding it that unionism can be said to have entered another phase of growth at all. While this phase of growth had a general character — that is, it represents both a recovery of the established trade unions and growth made through inroads into the organisation of the labour employed in the mass-production industries — it did represent a significant development in new directions to some extent in most countries. This proposition is quite clearly evident in the case of both the USA and Sweden, but was so closely interwoven with the growth of unionism throughout the period since 1914 in the UK and Australia that it cannot be identified as a distinctive development.

Table 2.1   Percentage of Eligible Labour Force
Unionised at Selected Dates in the UK, the USA,
Sweden and Australia

% Unionised

Date	UK	USA	Sweden	Australia
1900	12.7	5.5	N.A.	N.A.
1914	23.0	9.9	9.9	32.8
1920	45.2	16.7	26.3	42.2
1930	25.3	8.9	32.7	43.5
1939	31.6	14.9	48.3	39.2
1950	44.1	28.0	65.7	56.0
1960	43.1	26.3	70.9	54.5
1970	47.7	24.3	81.0	50.4*

Source: Computed from data in Tables E.1, E.2, E.3 and E.4
in Appendix E of Bain and Elsheikh (1976)

*Figure refers to 1969.

The fourth phase of growth involved the extension of unionism to the growing class of white-collar workers in the post-war period and proceeded quickly in most countries either immediately after the war or, as in the case of the USA, in the 1960s. In the years between 1950 and 1970 the table shows that unionism as a whole did not grow rapidly — it either stagnated or declined in each of the countries included in Table 2.1 except for Sweden. It may therefore seem paradoxical to call this a phase of growth. The answer to the paradox is provided by the very marked changes in the structure of the labour force which occurred in the post-war period. In particular the shift from manufacturing to service industry and the rapid growth of white-collar employment which has occurred in the post-war period in all the major industrial countries has narrowed the traditional base of union organisation and required unions to conquer new territory.

It is clear from the data in Table 2.1 that trade union growth in the twentieth century was substantial but erratic. There are a variety of factors which account for the particular patterns of growth observed in different countries but a significant factor in each of the countries considered above was the fluctuating level of economic activity. Other factors of importance were wars, political and social phenomena and the effects of legislation. (A detailed account of the determinants of the rate of growth of unionism is given in Bain and Elsheikh, 1976.)

In certain other countries, such as Germany, trade union growth was so affected by political events and wars that no long-period account of its determinants in economic terms can be given. In France and Italy trade union growth has been influenced to a very large extent by conflicts between communist and non-communist groups so that again it cannot be adequately accounted for as an economic phenomenon.

This description of union growth is not an account of why union growth occurred in the way that it has. In order to construct a general framework within which union growth can be analysed it is useful to think in terms of the demand for union services and the supply of union services and how these may have increased over time. Such a model is of limited value in providing a complete account of union growth due to the fact that the political and legislative environment within which trade unions have grown has had a profound influence on trade union growth independent of the demand and supply of union services.

Workers demand union services in the expectation of securing higher wages and to gain access to union representation in relation to non-wage issues in industrial relations such as job security, grievance procedures and disciplinary matters. As Ashenfelter and Johnson (1972) observe '. . . the purchase of unionism should be treated in part as an investment good and in part as a consumption good' (pp. 491–2). These same authors also cite extensive evidence that it is the 'consumption good' — access to union representation in non-wage issues — which is the predominant aspect of the demand for union services.

Now the purchase of union services involves workers in costs. The costs of buying union services include any initiation fees, union dues, possible employer hostility and a certain amount of trouble and inconvenience. If each worker was entirely free to decide whether to be a union member or not he would do so on the basis of deciding whether or not the returns to union membership were greater or less than the costs. In practice, of course, many workers are not entirely free to decide whether to join a union or not. Closed shops, union shops, pressure from other workers and so on all have the effect of making the decision to join a union or not simultaneous with entry to particular employments.

Consider how the demand for union services, which we assume to be normal good, may have increased over the period since unions were first established. First, the process of industrialisation had the initial effect of creating a complex system of industrial relations in which the individual worker and his employer became remote from each other and where the individual worker had little power to effectively represent his own interests. Over time this situation has probably become more acute as the scale and complexity of industry has increased and, on this view, the demand for union services has probably increased over time. The fact that the major phases of union growth have generally followed significant developments in the structure, scale or technology of industry lends some credibility to this notion. Second, it is commonly assumed that workers believe that unions are able to afford them some protection against adverse effects of market forces, particularly in respect of employment security and the growth of their real wages. Hence against the background of the recurrent depressions and price inflation which have characterised the last century we might expect increasing numbers of workers to decide that union membership was a price worth paying to obtain union protection. This proposition is well supported in the empirical literature. (See, for example, Ashenfelter and Pencavel 1969.) However, in order to account for any part of the general growth of unionism over time we must assume that workers do not dispense with union service in good times as readily as they acquire them in response to bad times. Third, the costs of union membership in terms of employer hostility have undoubtedly fallen over time as unionism has become increasingly accepted by employers. Moreover, the monetary cost of union membership in relation to real income has probably diminished over time. (See Roberts, 1962.) The supply of union services is determined by the costs of providing them — organisational costs, the costs of effectively representing member interests and the costs of extending unionism in the face of hostility from the public, employers and occasionally government. The returns are the benefits of extensive organisation. Again we might characterise the decision of a union to recruit an individual or to organise a workgroup in the aggregate as a straightforward cost/return equation. On this view the growth of unionism may be explained in part in terms of an increase in the supply of union services.

The costs of establishing a union in the first instance might be expected to be high relative to the marginal costs of expanding its membership once it is established, at least up to relatively high degrees of unionisation. This is simply a matter of scale economies. The overheads incurred in first establishing a viable union organisation can be spread over larger and larger numbers of workers and reduce the average costs of supplying union services although it has been argued that diminishing returns set in at some high degree of unionisation. (See Hines, 1964 and Rosen, 1969.) Moreover, it is arguable that the quality of the services supplied by unions has increased over time without corresponding increases in costs. As unions have grown they have achieved the status of major and influential economic institutions with the power to lobby effectively in respect of the policy of major employers and government. This has progressively extended the scope and importance of the services unions provide and is particularly apparent in the protection of member employment. Finally, after the era of initial recognition disputes had passed, the costs of further extensions of unionism, both monetary and psychological, presumably diminished. Hence on all these counts we might reasonably speculate that the supply of union services is likely to have grown over time.

The returns to an increase in the supply of union services are normally assumed to accrue in the form of advantages which unions derive from relatively high degrees of unionisation. There can be little doubt that many unions put a high priority on union growth. However certain small unions which have unionised most or all of the labour force in some particular employment, usually a single craft, show no desire to grow further. Turner (1962) has called the former group 'open unions' and the latter 'closed unions'. We shall return to these matters shortly.

The framework described above is useful in obtaining an overview of the spread of unionism over time. It is also a model of the process by which more detailed aspects of the structure and extent of unionism can be analysed and it commands empirical support. See Barbash (1956), Pencavel (1971) and McKersie and Brown (1963). We now proceed to examine the pattern of union growth and development in more detail.

The origins of unions

The exact origins of trade unions is obscure but it is well known that they evolved from 'friendly societies' of craftsmen. Their initial purposes were, *inter alia*, the maintenance of standards and *control over the rate of entry* into the craft. The main catalyst for this development was the growth of a class of craftsmen who were destined to remain employees throughout their working lives due to the increasing scale of viable workshop units implied by the emergence of an industrial society.

The investment in acquiring the skills of a craftsman, which typically was the passport to self-employed or employer status in the pre-industrial period, was increasingly viewed as a 'property' or 'vested interest' in the period of industrialisation. Hence workers banded themselves together in order to protect their 'property' from dilution by an influx of new entrants seeking to capitalise on the relatively high wages of craftsmen. A revealing example of this attitude is cited by Briggs (1964, p. 13) from the rule book of the Birmingham Wire Workers in 1869: 'The trade by which we live is our property, bought by certain years of servitude, which gives us a vested right, and we have an exclusive claim on it, as all will have hereafter who purchase it by the same means.' In effect then the purchase of union services was simultaneous with the purchase of the skill.

The rapid growth of demand for skilled craftsmen which accompanied the process of industrialisation made it necessary for the craft unions to control entry into the craft if property rights were to be protected and wages to remain high. The main instrument of control was the system of apprenticeship backed up by various forms of work regulation and the enforcement of minimum conditions and terms of employment throughout the craft. It is important to note that the early trade unions which pursued this type of policy were largely manipulating the supply of labour in order to influence the market wage (and to protect employment). This strategy of trade union activity is to be contrasted with 'power struggles' involving strikes which later became the main tactic of trade unions in collective bargaining.

Craft unions could afford to exploit their crucial economic position in the emerging economic order as a more or less sufficient means of protecting the wages and employment of their members. For the mass of unskilled workers who were drawn into the factory system in vast numbers as the scale and technology of industry raced ahead no such option was open. Huge reserves of unskilled labour existed in the agricultural sector of the economy and this made any strategy of union activity based on manipulation of labour supply impractible. In effect, economic circumstances had created a situation in which the mass of unskilled labour glutted the market and made even the maintenance of a 'living wage' extremely difficult. This is the sort of situation which typified the latter half of the nineteenth century in Britain and, to a lesser extent, the early 1920s in the USA.

Unskilled labour and unions

So long as ready substitutes existed for unskilled workers who attempted to improve their lot through trade union activity mass unionism could not get off the ground. The turning point in Britain came at the beginning of the 1890s which was the culmination of two decades in which the economic balance slowly shifted in favour of unskilled labour, as compared with the situation in the previous three decades, and in which trade unionism had grown steadily in a number of a non-craft employments such as mining and textiles. In the early 1890s a number of strikes amongst unorganised workers — the most famous being the 'docker's tanner' strike of 1891 — took place and trade unionism got a foothold amongst unskilled labour. There were many factors which led to this development – changes in the economic, political, legislative and industrial climate together with the example of the craft and non-craft unions which had resorted to strike activity. However a central feature of the emergence of mass unionism was the acquisition by unskilled workers of sufficient economic power to conduct an effective strike and prevent employers from eroding the strike by substitution of non-union labour. The fact that the newborn unions of unskilled labour were virtually wiped out within a matter of three years due to a severe economic depression is witness to the importance of this factor.

The foregoing account of the origins and early development of trade unions places much emphasis on the economic factors which were at work. This is of course a deliberate attempt to highlight the economic elements which formed the background to the emergence of unionism. Many people would dispute that economic factors had a major role in the origins of trade unionism and would point to social, political and broad historical developments as the motivating forces. We do not deny the importance of these factors but choose instead to emphasise the the economic context which appears to provide a significant part of any account of the origins of trade unionism.

Hence by the end of the nineteenth century one could view the trade union movement, then two million strong in Britain and comprising many non-craft workers, as having achieved its initial success '. . . in proportion as it resisted the temptation to go counter to the economic forces of the times; and has directed its chief efforts to giving men a new spirit and a trust in and care for one another; and inciting them to avail themselves of these economic forces that can be made to work on their side' (Alfred Marshall, 1920). Craft unionism became established because the unions were able to capitalise on the tightness of the labour market for their members and because they were able to control entry into the craft by means of the apprenticeship system.

In addition, the craft unions were careful to preserve their individual identity so that the boundaries of their jurisdiction were clearly defined and recognised and served to protect their members' exclusive rights to practise their craft. Hence, the network of demarcation rules which persist in British industry derives from conventions designed by the craft unions in the 19th century to establish control over the whole range of jobs within the craft.

The general and industrial unions which later organised the non-craft workers were only able to do so half a century after the foundation of the craft unions when the balance of supply and demand created the conditions under which successful strikes could be undertaken and further growth in their membership achieved. We shall return to this latter issue in an analytical context in chapter 6.

Trade unionism had therefore become *established* in Britain by the turn of the century. While there remained many legal and industrial battles to be fought before British unions could truly regard their activities as being accepted facts of industrial life, their continued existence was not seriously in jeopardy after 1900. Hence we might identify a period in which unions fought to establish their right to exist — which roughly corresponds with the first phase of growth — followed by a 'take-off' period in which unions grew in membership and also progressively consolidated their right to function as industrial and economic institutions. The take-off period occurred at different times in different countries but it is evident from a detailed examination of the growth pattern of unionism that some such process occurred in almost all countries at one or more points in time. (See Davis (1941), Ross (1948), Dunlop (1950) and Levinson (1967) for more detailed discussion of this issue.)

Within the broad features which characterise the take-off period in union development there is a story of great complexity which has varied widely from time to time and from country to country. The growth of trade union membership has fluctuated massively from time to time and crucial legal battles and strikes have been fought by unions and these have often altered the whole course of their development. These are the meat of the history of trade unionism. It is, however, no part of our purpose to document trade union history in any detail so the interested reader is referred to Flanders and Clegg (1964) and to Reynolds (1964) for accounts of the history of unionism in Britain and the USA respectively. There are two matters however to which we must address ourselves in the context of trade union development; the structure of trade unions and the non-wage activities of union.

Trade union structure

We have already noted that craft unions of skilled tradesmen were the first to emerge. Craft unionism therefore became established as the earliest element of the trade union structure and has survived in one form or another to this day in Britain, North America and some European countries. Initially the craft unions tended to be formed on a local basis, bringing together all the craftsmen in a particular trade in a city, part of a city or a group of towns. However, since it was a major objective of craft unionism to establish uniform minimum conditions of work and pay throughout the craft, a national structure which united the local unions emerged as unionism matured. In Britain the local identity of the original craft unions has tended to become completely submerged in the national structure but in the USA union locals still retain a certain autonomy from their national organisations. In most other countries pure craft unions are rare.

Many craft unions did not retain their craft identity at either local or national level as the trade union movement developed. In countries such as Sweden, Holland and Germany craft unionism was largely eliminated by a deliberate restructuring of the trade union movements on the basis of industrial unionism. Industrial unions limit their jurisdiction to a single industry (usually defined in relation to its product market) and embrace all workers irrespective of their skill or grade. Industrial unionism has always had a special attraction since it is at once neat and tidy and focused on the whole of an industry so that the potential for product market substitution against the unionised sector is restricted. Most 'industrial' unions in Britain (there are few 'pure' cases) are the result of mergers between a number of unions operating within the same industry which saw strength in unity but in the USA industrial unions emerged as part of a deliberate strategy designed to organise the mass production industries in the 1920s. In Continental Europe industrial unionism is the norm in all countries except for France and Italy and is the result of a process of restructuring intended to streamline the trade union movement and reduce the total number of unions. In most cases — e.g. Germany and Holland — this was done in the process of reorganising the trade union movements which had been suppressed during the Second World War, but in the Scandinavian countries was the result of a more or less voluntary desire on the part of the trade union movements to tidy up their structure.

General unionism is the third main category of union structure and one form exists in Britain while different forms exist in France and Italy. In Britain the great influx of unskilled labour into trade unions at the end of the nineteenth century could not have been contained within the craft unions and, since industrial unionism was unknown at that time, a haphazard growth of unions which accepted all comers was the vehicle by which the trade union movement responded to its sudden growth. These general unions sprawl across many industries and occupations but are normally structured internally in such a way as to reflect the natural groupings which they embrace. In the USA there are a number of unions which are to all intents and purposes 'general' unions and these are mainly craft type unions which have broadened their membership in the interests of growth. In France and Italy syndicalism — which prescribes one large union for all workers — was an important element in the early development of the trade union movements in these countries and has led to a situation in which all-embracing federations of unions form the basic structure of the trade union movement. Additionally, in those countries there exists a dominant communist federation and rival socialist and Christian federations.

The determinants of trade union structure are very varied as between countries. In Britain the growth of the trade union movement has been a series of haphazard responses to unexpected or unmanageable developments — in the words of Turner (1955) the guiding principle of British trade union development has been that '. . . nature abhors a vacuum'. There exist in Britain today about 600 separate trade unions of every size, shape and political complexion and this has led to a most complex and often chaotic system of workers' representation. In the USA two distinct groups of unions operate side by side within a general alliance. The craft unions, which were initially associated with the American Federation of Labour (AFL), and the industrial unions which were originally associated with the Congress of Industrial Organisation (CIO), all fall within the umbrella of the central federation, the AFL/CIO, but still retain much of their original identity and policies. The unions in Continental Europe (except France and Italy) are compact alliances of industrial unions while in France and Italy unwieldy and expressly political federations are dominant.

Now the structure of the trade union movement is the outcome of an evolutionary process which occurred after the initial phase of development and consolidation. Once unions had gained a toehold in industry and were able to engage in effective collective bargaining their continuing existence was more or less guaranteed and the energies which had hitherto been directed mainly towards survival were deployed in part to improving their structure, both as a movement and as an internal organisational process. In some countries, particularly Britain, structural change was very much an unplanned and *ad hoc* process based on trade union mergers, the creation of alliances (federations) and the absorption of small unions by big ones. In other countries an element of conscious planning was instrumental in developing the structure of the trade union movement and in the Scandinavian, Dutch and German cases restructuring was undertaken as a method of total reorganisation. The economic implications of trade union structure are of interest here. (For a detailed account of institutional aspects of union structure see Turner, 1955.

Economic aspects of union structure

We have already noted that craft unions were able to achieve certain economic objectives by the manipulation of the supply of labour. This special power of craft unions could only be effectively preserved by preserving the jurisdictional integrity of the union and the retention of all of the apparatus of control of entry. However, in Europe, an ethic embracing egalitarianism, the unity of the working class and the political role of organised labour militated strongly against the retention of a separate identity for the 'elite' craft unions. In contrast, in the USA, where the ethic of 'business unionism' (which argues that unions should act in broadly the same manner as a business enterprise) was prevalent, craft unionism had a distinct rationale to support its elitist role. Indeed a fierce dispute raged throughout the 1920s and 1930s in the USA as to the appropriate role of craft unionism within the organised labour movement and the AFL conceded not an inch. The balance between craft unionism on the one hand, and industrial unionism on the other was therefore largely struck in each country according to the political orientation of the trade union movement.

The economic issues involved in union structure are fairly straightforward. Skilled craftsmen, because of their ability to control entry to their trade and some other reasons discussed in chapter 5, can wield exceptional power through the apparatus of craft unionism. In particular, the members of craft unions could be expected to increase their own wages relative to those of other workers and to provide for greater security of employment than other workers over time. Industrial and general unions on the other hand must operate wholly on the basis of the exercise of extensive power based on strikes and strike threats. In general the economic power implied by this mode of operation is rather less than that of craft unions. (See chapter 6). From a purely selfish economic point of view therefore the members of craft unions have a vested interest in remaining apart from the rest of the labour force. Trade union movements however have always been characterised by political motivations and the craft unions have often been under pressure to surrender their independence in the interest of the greater good of the trade union movement — in other words they should permit their special economic power to be harnessed by the remainder of the labour force so that organised labour as a whole will benefit as a result.

The classification of unions into craft, industrial and general categories is a convenient method of describing trade union structure. However, Turner (1962) has questioned the appropriateness of such a classification in functional terms. Certain unions which started out as craft unions — such as the Amalgamated Engineering Union in Britain and the International Brotherhood of Electrical Workers in the USA — soon developed an appetite for extensive organisation and their members are now drawn from a wide variety of crafts and skills. In most cases of this kind an economic motive lay behind the growth of the craft unions beyond their original jurisdictions. For example many craft unions found that the only effective method of preventing the substitution of helpers or journeymen for craftsmen in the event of a strike was to absorb them into the union. Once a process of this kind is set in motion it is inclined to take on a momentum of its own and the union eventually ceases, in effect, to be a craft union. Similarly, industrial unions such as the National Union of Railwaymen in Britain and the United Automobile Workers in the USA have recruited into their membership workers from outside the industry.

When craft, and to a lesser extent, industrial unions, organise outside of their traditional jurisdiction they often find it necessary to expand further and further into alien territory to progressively limit the potential for either labour or product substitution against their members. Growth therefore becomes a central objective of union policy and the union effectively trades its ability to restrict entry into the occupations which it organises for the bargaining power which extensive organisation confers on it. The economic logic which underlies this strategy is discussed fully in chapter 3. Unions which pursue expansionist policies are called 'open' unions by Turner and this is a characterisation of union type which we will have occasion to use as we proceed.

In contrast to the expansionist policies of the open unions, other unions have found it expedient to maintain their control over entry into the employments within their jurisdiction and to pursue restrictionist policies. Examples of such unions are the Boilermakers' Society in Britain and in the USA locals in the building and printing trades. Such unions are not necessarily 'craft' unions in the conventional sense — they may organise workers of relatively little skill or highly qualified workers in the professions — but they are characterised by the restrictionist policies and entry controls of the traditional craft unions. Hence these unions are called 'closed' unions and typically they are relatively small, with a stable membership and no expansionist ambitions. The economic rationale of the closed union lies in its ability to retain its exclusive character and thereby ensure that the balance of supply and demand for its members' services can be manipulated in the economic interests of its members.

The point of this exercise is to provide a basis for analysing the economic aspects of trade union activity in terms of the structural characteristics of unions. Open unions behave differently from closed unions in terms of their economic policies and so we must distinguish between them in analysis. The conventional distinction between craft, industrial and general unions is often not an economically useful one nowadays so that we shall frequently refer to unions as either closed or open instead. Hence, whatever the nominal classification of a union, we call all the general unions and those craft and industrial unions which do not pursue policies of general restriction on entry, open unions, and those unions which pursue general restrictive-entry policies, closed unions.

The emergence in the post-war period of large-scale white-collar unionism is the most dramatic recent structural development in the trade union movements of most industrial countries. In the USA — where white-collar unionism is only significant amongst government employees — a new generation of specifically white-collar unions was established. In Britain white-collar unionism has made significant inroads into the private as well as the public sector and in many instances already-established blue-collar unions have organised the white-collar workers by establishing white-collar affiliates. However, exclusively white-collar unions also exist and certain of them were established as early as 1919. White-collar unionism does not however raise any particular issues which require to be dealt with outside the context of the general economic analysis of unions. The tendency to single white-collar unions out for special treatment in the industrial relations literature results from their distinctive institutional character-istics but these generally do not have an economic counterpart so that we shall have no need to treat white-collar unionism as a distinctive economic phenomenon.

The internal structure of unions

Unions vary greatly in their internal structure and it is not part of our purpose to describe their internal structure in any detail. (See Flanders and Clegg (1964) chapter 3 and Reynolds (1964) for a full account of internal union structure.) However there is an aspect of the internal structure of unions which is worthy of some general comment.

By and large unions have tended over the years to organise their internal structure of authority in line with that of the management decision-making process. Hence, at one end of the scale we have national union officials dealing with top management and at the other end we have shop stewards dealing with supervisors or foremen. From the point of view of the union this is an eminently sensible form of internal organisation but management have frequently viewed it with distrust since it has the potential to erode management prerogatives.

In some cases it may have been a deliberate union policy to construct a system of representation which parallels that of the structure of management decision making but it often appears as though it was a spontaneous and unplanned response to the growing depth of union activity. Management have generally responded to this development by trying to formalise it within non-bargaining channels of representation such as joint-consultative machinery and works councils of one kind or another which exist in almost all the industrialised countries except the USA and Britain. In Britain and the USA management have normally tried to contain the influence of unions at lower levels of decision making by formalising bargaining at those levels through written agreements and accepted procedures. The degree to which they have succeeded in doing so varies from plant to plant. The main point of interest for our purpose in the British case is that the internal structure of union representation gives rise to a hierarchy of bargaining units each with the potential to act as a channel of union economic influence. Ultimately bargaining structure can be described and analysed in terms of a complex of collective bargaining units and we examine this phenomenon in chapters 7 and 8.

There is little more to be gained by further discussion of trade union structure except to note that each trade union movement has some type of central representative body. In Britain it is the Trades Union Congress, in the USA the AFL/CIO, in Sweden the LO, and so on. Generally these congresses have as their aim the co-ordination of the policies of their individual affiliates and certain functions in respect of trade union relations with governments and central employer organisations. Their effectiveness depends on the degree to which they can command the support of their affiliates and this in turn depends on the degree to which their affiliates are prepared to surrender their autonomy to a congress. It is sufficient to note that the authority of congresses varies considerably. In Sweden the LO is very powerful and engages in collective bargaining on behalf of its affiliates, in Britain the TUC has had mixed fortunes in its attempts to formulate effective general policies but in recent years has, with the backing of Labour government, managed to carry its affiliates into various forms of pay policy.

The significance of the relationship of a trade union congress to its affiliates clearly lies in the degree to which individual trade union policies are influenced by the policy of the congress.

Unions and non-wage objectives

We have already recognised that the economic environment was only one element in the process by which trade unions evolved. What we must note however is that as trade unions developed they became major economic institutions and assumed functions in relation to worker/employer relations which went beyond the simple matter of wage-fixing. In representing their members' interests, unions took on the function of regulating the general relations between their members and the employers.

Hence unions concerned themselves in the whole range of non-wage issues in industrial relations. Conditions of work, rules of employment, grievance procedures, health and safety at work and matters of discipline all became matters on which unions assumed a representative function on behalf of their members. Moreover as unions matured during the 20th century these non-wage issues became an increasingly important part of the business of trade unions. It is true to say that the majority of trade union resources and energy today are devoted to the regulation of non-wage issues and it is important that this is recognised.

Relations between workers and employers span a vast spectrum of issues ranging from trivial disputes between an individual worker and a supervisor on the shop floor to major confrontations at national level over such issues as closed-shop agreements. Over the years unions and employers have established procedures for dealing with disputes — wage and non-wage — at all levels at which decision making occurs. There now exists within industry a vast complex of rules, regulations and procedures which govern the behaviour of both employers and unions in respect of almost every aspect of industrial relations. Through these regulations unions seek to protect the interest of their members in a comprehensive way but particularly in order to limit the scope for arbitrary action by employers. Examples of such activity on the part of unions which are of current significance in Britain are in respect of redundancies (lay-offs), participation in management decision making, dismissals, discrimination against women and minorities, disciplinary action and issues involved in the innovation of new technology.* Needless to say, the existence of such a wide spectrum of issues presents itself to the union to some extent as a trade-off — that is, the union can choose to make advances on certain issues at the expense of others according to its strategy and this may involve a trade-off between economic and non-economic issues in some circumstances.

It was, of course, an entirely natural process of evolution which led trade unions to broaden their horizons from the initial economic base which provided the rationale for their foundation. As trade unionism spread and became more powerful in industry the unions progressively took on the functions which politicians, philanthropists and the state had undertaken in earlier times. Similarly, at factory and workshop level, where the growing scale of industry and the emergence of a new class of wealthy factory owners had created a great gulf in relations between worker and employer, the union became the natural

---

*Many of these issues are, of course, subject to regulation by law and the influence of unions on the development of industrial relations law has been significant. However, many issues are not specifically covered by legislation and, in any case, many grey areas remain.

intermediary, providing a channel of communication between worker and employer which was both immediate and professional. Hence although the trade union movement originated primarily to advance the economic interests of its members it quickly absorbed many functions which were not entirely economic in their content.

We now proceed to sketch in some of the more fundamental questions about the nature of trade unionism by reference to a celebrated debate between Arthur Ross (1948) and John Dunlop (1950) on the subject. In many respects the central theme of this debate concerns the validity of the subject matter of this whole book — whether or not economic analysis is an appropriate tool for the analysis of trade union activity.

The nature of trade unions: Ross versus Dunlop

We have already seen that political and economic factors are inextricably linked to each other in the activities of trade unions. So far we have taken the view that, despite the ambivalence of the trade union as an institution, an economic account of many of their activities and the influences which shaped their development is a useful way of understanding their behaviour. This indeed was the orthodox economic position prior to the Second World War. In 1948 Arthur Ross launched a frontal assault on the economic orthodoxy by characterising unions as political institutions operating in an economic environment. He disputed that the standard assumptions and methods of economic analysis were capable of providing a useful understanding of trade union activity. We shall characterise Ross's position in a highly simplified and brief way and then describe Dunlop's defence of the role of economic analysis.

Ross's view

Ross begins by declaring that '. . . . we no longer have a satisfactory theory of wages' and proceeds to argue that this is a consequence of assuming that trade unions could be treated within wage theory as rational economic agents seeking to maximise some economic variable or variables. (It is worth pointing out that certain of the anomalies in wage theory which Ross cites in support of the assertion above have been made irrelevant by the development of human capital theory.) According to Ross the position of union leaders is critical to union wage policies. The union is made up of a heterogeneous set of members with heterogeneous interests. For example we might identify some heterogeneous groups within a union's membership — older workers, young workers, black workers, white workers, men and women, married and unmarried and militant and non-militant. Older workers may be much more concerned with such issues as retirement age, pension provisions and seniority rules than with current wages while young workers may put current wages above all else in their list of priorities. In any event it is likely that a great variety of different pressures will emerge from the rank and file membership of a union and impress themselves on the union leader as the varied aspirations of the people he is paid to represent.

It is the job of the union leader to satisfy his membership. Whether he is elected or appointed his job may depend on his ability to satisfy his members. Indeed, since other unions may well be in competition for the allegiance of his members, the very survival of the union may depend on the ability of the union leader to satisfy his members. The problem facing the union leader therefore is how to reconcile the various pressures brought to bear on him by the various factions within his union's membership. In many instances the issue is amenable to compromise but in others there may be open conflict and the union leader must seek to follow the course which does least harm to his position and that of the union as an institution. He may, for example, be faced with a demand for a sharp increase in pensions by the older workers and a sharp increase in wages by the younger workers and know that he cannot have both. Compromise may be possible or it may not but, in any case, the union leader must respond to the most immediate and relevant pressure. If old men dominate the union then pensions will be given priority but if the future is perceived to lie in pleasing the younger workers then wages will get priority.

The foregoing is something of a caricature of Ross's position but nevertheless what we are describing is essentially a *political* decision-making process. This is the nub of Ross's argument – union wage policy formulated on the basis of a process by which a host of political pressures are reconciled by the union leadership and this cannot generally be described as rational economic maximising behaviour as it is characterised in orthodox neo-classical economic analysis.

It follows from this that unions will pursue objectives and behave in ways that appear irrational by the criteria of orthodox economics. Irrational economic behaviour is a phenomenon which orthodox economic analysis is poorly equipped to explain even though such behaviour may be *politically* rational. Hence trade unions cannot usefully be subjected to economic analysis but instead must be understood in terms of a political analysis.

Dunlop's response

Dunlop rejected Ross's argument in a book published in 1950 (Dunlop, 1950) on the basis of four main grounds. First, Dunlop argued that the dominance of political factors in union wage policy was a feature of a small number of new unions in which factional infighting had occurred – it was not an accurate representation of the bulk of unions. Second, political considerations are essentially short-run aspects of union wage policy – in the long run economic forces determine wage/employment outcomes. Third, it is misleading to assume that union leaders are preoccupied with political considerations – in fact they are economically literate and behave in accordance with the economic facts of life. Fourth, internal union political decision making is only one aspect of a much more complex process of wage fixing and it is a matter of fact that the behaviour of wages can be well explained by market variables. Dunlop then proceeds to offer a model of trade union behaviour in which unions are postulated to maximise their membership in respect of a wage/membership function. Dunlop's model is outlined in chapter 3 so that we shall not take his case further at this point.

A view of the Ross—Dunlop debate

Our view of this disagreement may be summarised as follows. Union leaders are subject to a host of internal pressures emanating from factions within the union — including those within the leadership — and other pressures which are external to the union and policy formulation must take the form of striking delicate and complex balances between competing pressures in order to maintain some kind of internal and external equilibrium. This is the essential 'political' element in the decision-making process and is viewed by Ross as the dominant feature of policy formulation. However, when all the internal political decision making has been completed and an economic policy adopted it must take the form of *specific* packages of wage claims and claims relating to the terms and conditions of employment. These packages, independent of how rational the process of constructing them was, become manifest as simple economic variables which are in turn subject to the laws of the economic system. In other words, the union must determine its priorities internally and we must accept that, for the union, its package of claims is a utility-maximising one and analyse its economic implications accordingly. Hence, at a global level, we are more sympathetic to the view of Dunlop but see merit in the insights provided by Ross so long as they are contained within a model of the internal decision-making process which precedes the process by which the key economic variables are adjusted. The point here is that while the utility-maximising behaviour of the union may not be 'rational' in the conventional economic sense, because it is determined by political considerations, it remains perfectly legitimate to employ the tools of economic analysis to understand the activities of the union. Moreover the external economic constraints imposed by the market on the ability of the union to manipulate economic variables remain effective whether or not the union is 'rational' or not so that, in terms of economic *outcomes*, the effect of the union on the economy is quite amenable to analysis of a fairly conventional kind.

We shall return from time to time to certain aspects of the Ross/Dunlop debate where it is relevant in gaining a better insight into particular issues but we now proceed on the assumption that economic analysis is relevant to an understanding of trade union activity.

Summary

In order to undertake an economic analysis of trade unions we must have a general view of their origins, structure and development. Trade unions originated in most countries in the form of local unions of craftsmen who, because they could control entry to their trade, could manipulate the supply of labour to their economic advantage. Unskilled workers possessed no economic power of the kind that craftsmen did. Hence unionism generally only extended to unskilled labour when labour market conditions swung in their favour and some catalyst — such as a strike or a political phenomenon — was introduced to the situation.

Economic factors were an important dimension of the environment in which trade unions developed but as unions matured the scope of their activities broadened considerably to embrace a great many non-economic issues. This process has continued and modern unions now probably devote as much time and resources to representing their members in relation to grievances, rights and other non-wage issues as they do to wholly economic issues. Hence in applying the tools of economic analysis to the study of trade unions we must bear in mind the broader context in which unions operate.

Trade union structure is of interest as an aspect of the developmental process of unionism and also because it has economic implications. Craft unionism, which was the forerunner of other forms of unionism, endows craftsmen with relatively great economic power. However, considerations of equity, solidarity and the objectives of socialism have led to the absorption of craft unions into industrial unions in a number of European countries but craft unions have survived very effectively in the USA and less effectively in Britain. Nowadays it is more useful to think in terms of a distinction between 'closed' and 'open' unions for the purposes of economic analysis. Closed unions operate in much the same way as traditional craft unions but not all so-called craft unions are closed. Open unions derive their power from extensive organisation and most industrial, some craft and all general unions are open. The internal structure and organisation of trade unions is also of economic relevance. In general, unions have devised internal structures which permit levels of union authority to correspond to levels of management decision making. This development has inevitably given rise to a situation in which unions have become increasingly involved in the decision-making process in industry — a development which management has frequently tried to contain or formalise within channels of communications which have clearly-defined limits.

Finally, we have introduced the debate between Arthur Ross and John Dunlop which concerns the nature of trade unions. Ross gave great prominence to the union as an institution and the political character of decision making within the union which springs from the interaction of a heterogeneous membership and a union leadership which must respond to the various pressures which emanate from that membership. Ross concluded that the decisions on policy matters which the leader of a union would be obliged to take would reflect the reconciliation of political pressures and generally be 'irrational' in terms of economic analysis. On this view therefore union activity cannot be usefully subjected to conventional economic analysis.

Dunlop's response to Ross, with which we are in broad agreement, was that unions do have a political dimension but it is not nearly so pervasive as Ross asserts. Unions exist in an economic environment and many of their objectives require them to influence economic variables. Union leaders are aware of the economic realities which they face in pursuing any economic policy and generally behave in a way which reflects that awareness. In any case, whatever the inspiration for a union's economic policy, it will have predictable consequences which are quite amenable to economic analysis and that is a major part of our purpose in this book.

Further reading

A. Flanders and H. Clegg (eds) *The System of Industrial Relations in Great Britain* Oxford, Blackwell (1964).
A. Rees *The Economics of Trade Unions* University of Chicago Press (1962).
L. G. Reynolds *Labor Economics and Labor Relations* Englewood Cliffs N.J., Prentice-Hall (1964).

CHAPTER 3

Union Wage Policy

In any economy in which the trade unions do not have the whole labour force in membership we must distinguish between union labour and non-union labour. Amongst the non-communist countries of the world there are none in which trade union membership is coextensive with the labour force, so that non-union labour is part of the labour force in the cases in which we are interested. We must, though, be careful here. Non-union labour may be defined as that part of the labour force not in union membership. However, as we shall see, many non-union workers are affected in various economic ways by the activities of trade unions, and a sharp conceptual distinction between union and non-union labour sometimes cannot be made. But for the moment we shall assume that a sharp distinction between union members and non-union members is possible and modify this assumption later.

The supply of labour in the short run

The short-run analysis of labour supply normally focuses on the individual or the family unit as a supplier of hours of work in a competitive labour market. Fleisher (1970) deals with this question in detail, so we shall only briefly consider it here.

The conventional theory views the individual as an economic agent choosing between two goods, income (work) and leisure (income forgone). The units of measurement are pay and hours. Hence, since a day is limited to 24 hours, an individual may choose, within that constraint, any combination of hours worked and not worked according to his preferences for income and leisure. (We shall ignore the complication that income and leisure may be interdependent and assume that they are independent.) In the same way as a consumer is portrayed in microeconomic theory as choosing between two goods, the analysis of labour supply proceeds by reference to utility maps made up of indifference curves between income and leisure. Each indifference curve is a locus of combinations of hours worked and hours not worked between which the individual is indifferent. Since income and leisure are assumed to be normal goods the indifference curves are convex to the origin. The 'budget line' in this case is the relative price of hours supplied, i.e. the wage rate.

Fig. 3.1

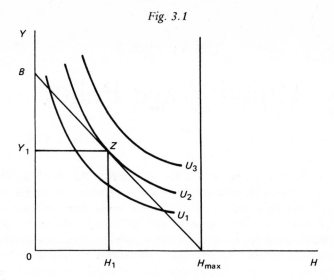

Figure 3.1 illustrates the simplest possible situation. The individual's utility function is expressed in the shape of the indifference curves U_1, U_2 and U_3 (which are selected from an infinite set) and the configuration of his indifference map. The further to the north-east that a curve lies in the map, the higher the level of utility it represents. Now the wage rate is given by the slope of the line BH_{max} and the individual maximises utility by equating the hourly wage rate with the marginal rate of substitution between income and leisure, i.e. the slope of an indifference curve. Utility is maximised at point Z where the slope of the budget line (the hourly wage rate) is equal to the slope of the highest attainable indifference curve (the marginal rate of substitution between income and leisure), which in this case is U_2. This means that the individual who is faced with the choice set implied by the budget line BH_{max} and whose utility function is described by the indifference map $U_1 \ldots U_3$ will maximise his utility by working OH_1 hours, for which he receives an income of OY_1, and enjoying leisure of H_{max} minus H_1 hours. In this case then, given the wage rate, the individual will supply OH_1 hours and that is a typical example of the short-run supply decision of any individual. Complications of various kinds normally enter this analysis owing to the fact that some hours are paid for at premium rates, some individuals have non-work incomes, wages and hours may be simultaneously determined and some individuals may do more than one job, but the essential analysis of short-run labour supply is as portrayed in our simple case.

Typically this type of analysis views the wage rate as given so that the only choice available to the individual is the number of hours supplied at that rate.* It is true that the analysis can readily show how individuals will alter their

---

*The implications of a variable wage rate and fixed hours, and variable wages and hours, are discussed by Gordon (1976).

supply of hours when the wage rate changes, but it is normally implicitly assumed that wage changes are exogenous and beyond the control of the individual. Clearly any theory of the supply of hours of work by the members of a trade union cannot be cast in such a restrictive mould.

The supply of hours of work by union labour

The above analysis refers to any *individual* and cannot be aggregated for a group of individuals since each individual is assumed to have a set of tastes and preferences which are particular to him and aggregation of individual utility functions is therefore impossible. In the interests of simplicity, however, we may assume for a moment that some group of individuals is homogeneous in utility functions and that we may aggregate the functions in such a way that the example contained in fig. 3.1 represents the utility-maximising decision of the group rather than of an individual. Now if the members of the group decide to form themselves into a trade union and appoint one of their members as president how will the situation change?

The union president will judge that the union must attempt to increase the utility of its members over what they enjoyed before becoming unionised, if the union is to yield net returns to them. He must therefore construct a *trade union utility function* which, when maximised, will yield the membership a higher level of utility than before. But he now has problems because he is faced with the task of maximising the collective utility of the union membership. The president can seek to do this either by increasing the income they receive from the same number of hours of work as they supplied before they were unionised or by reducing hours of work supplied while maintaining their income at the same level as before unionisation. In both cases this requires an increase in the wage rate. We noted that in the analysis of the individual or non-union group case the wage rate tends to be taken as given and only the number of hours supplied is a matter of effective choice. In the case of a union, maximising the union's utility function requires the wage rate to be open to change by the activity of the union.

The supply of men

The short-run theory of the supply of hours of work therefore predicts that unions will only be able to increase their members' utility by increasing the wage rate. But we must rephrase the argument in terms of the supply of *men* rather than supply of hours of work. This is so because with a group of individuals we are dealing with discrete blocks of hours of work supplied as well as with marginal adjustments in the supply of hours within any individual block. Moreover, from the point of view of a trade union its membership comprises men rather than hours supplied, and from the point of view of an employer the unit of labour supply is a man even though the hours bought from each man at the margin is the crucial variable. Hence we are simply consolidating our analysis of the supply of hours of work into the supply of men, who are the units which supply those hours, while still retaining the assumption that each individual is free to supply hours of work at the margin according to his own utility function. Now this redefinition of labour supply has two important practical implications.

First, our union president is no longer able to conceive of his job simply as to increase his members' utility by increasing their wage rate and allowing each to adjust his supply of hours according to his own utility function. Since his members are discrete blocks of hours supplied, adjustments in total hours supplied by them may only be possible by increasing or reducing the number of supplying units. For example, an increase in the wage rate may increase the number of hours which the employed membership are prepared to supply but may also require other men to enter the employment if the total increase in hours demanded exceeds the number which the original employed group are prepared to supply. Similarly, a fall in the wage rate may decrease the number of hours which the employed group are prepared to supply but such an adjustment may only be possible by reducing the numbers of men supplying them. This is so because there are in practice constraints on the ability of a given number of supplying units (men) to increase or decrease their supply of hours and — dropping our assumption of homogeneous utility functions — different preferences in different individuals.

The factors which restrict increases in individual hours supplied are obvious — ultimately a day is only 24 hours long and individuals must have time to sleep, eat, etc. The main constraint on reducing hours supplied by individuals is that employers normally require some minimum average number of hours. These constraints will introduce discontinuities into the individual's utility function and often result in sub-optimal decisions being made. However, they are facts of life and may characterise the whole range of employment possibilities open to certain individuals as inevitably leading to sub-optimal situations.

The particular importance of this for our union president is that any changes in wages which he is able to obtain for his members may involve a change in the number of members he has in the union and may also raise the question of *which* of his members he should favour in seeking to change wage rates. This is the first complication of the president's task — there are many others connected with this same issue.

Secondly, if the union president can only increase the utility of his membership by increasing the wage rate above that which obtained before the union was formed, it is likely that outsiders — non-union labour — will be attracted to seek employment and this will threaten to undermine the union-won wage increase. Again this is a problem which is revealed only when the supply of labour is conceived of as men rather than hours. The complication

facing the union president now is how to protect the union-won wage increase against the competition from non-union labour. This issue is usually resolved by devices such as job-rationing, closed shops or union shops or other restrictions on the entry of non-union labour into an employment.

Our union president now recognises that in order to increase the utility of his members he must secure increased wages for them, must control the resulting increases or decreases in the membership and must protect the union-won wage increase against competition from non-union labour. The task of being a union president is evidently a complicated one. Let us now go on to consider the kind of utility function which the union president will adopt as a working hypothesis in seeking to increase the utility of his members.

The union's utility function

Since we are interested in the economic aspects of trade union activity we shall confine our attention to the main economic variables likely to enter into the union's utility function.

Note first of all that we are talking of the *union's* utility function here. Thus we are implying that the union president must determine what is an appropriate collective utility function for his membership. Now, unless the membership have homogeneous utility functions, which we shall henceforth assume they do not, the job of the union president is to identify a utility function which will reflect the broadest possible balance of tastes and preferences of all his members. This may prove difficult in practice since there may be factions within the union with distinct tastes and preferences — such as the older workers who may be concerned particularly with such things as pensions, retirement age, etc. — and these factions may vary considerably in their power to influence union policy. Hence the union president may have to attach different weights to the aspirations of different groups within the union, and this can only be done at the expense of the least influential groups (A. M. Ross, 1948, has discussed this matter in detail). To recognise that a union president must strike a balance between competing interest groups within the union in formulating its policy is to begin to view the union as an institution which may have an identity and a motivation transcending that of the average of its members.

Bearing in mind the possibility that a union may have its own 'institutional' identity let us try to identify the main objectives which the union president will seek to achieve. First, and most obvious, he will wish to increase the wage rate of his members over the level at which the market would have set it. He will not, however, wish to increase wage rates without limit since the demand for labour is invariably somewhat elastic and this will constrain his wage ambitions. Secondly, he will wish to ensure a high level of employment amongst his members. Again this is a desire which is constrained by the fact that the demand for labour is always elastic in some measure. Let us consider the implications of

Fig. 3.2

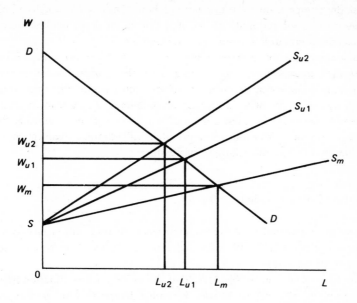

these two objectives and the constraints imposed by a less than completely inelastic demand for labour.

Consider some given demand curve for labour which is negatively sloped and the options it presents to the union president. In fig. 3.2 we illustrate a situation in which there is demand curve *DD* — which is of the conventional negatively sloped type — and a market supply curve of labour S_m which is (also by convention) positively sloped. The wage rate is measured on the vertical axis and numbers of men on the horizontal axis. Before the labour force was unionised the supply of labour would have been described by the line SS_m, the wage would have been fixed at OW_m and employment would have been OL_m.

When the labour force is unionised the union must establish a higher wage for its members than the competitive wage. Hence the union will wish to raise the supply price of its members to the employer by operating with reference to a supply curve like SS_{u1} or SS_{u2}. (We are assuming for simplicity that the reservation wage is *OS* for union and non-union labour alike.) Now it may readily be seen in fig. 3.2 that the higher the wage which the union secures for its members, the fewer men the employer will be prepared to hire. The demand curve *DD* therefore acts as a constraint on the ability of the union to pursue its wage and employment objectives simultaneously. We call this a 'trade-off' between wages and employment, and this concept can be developed to depict the union's utility function as a map of indifference curves. Each indifference curve is a locus of combinations of wage rates and employment levels which yield a constant level of utility to the union. Figure 3.3 is an example of a union's

Fig. 3.3

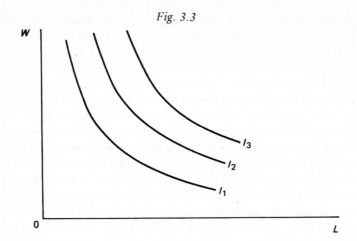

utility map where wages and employment are the only elements in the union's utility function.

The utility map of a union will vary from case to case both in the shape and in the configuration of the indifference curves. Some unions will attach a great deal of weight to employment objectives and less to wage objectives while other unions will do the opposite. Also, different unions will place different weights on the desirability of increasing wages and increasing employment as movements through the indifference map occur (in response to changes in labour demand). The sort of factors which determine the union's utility function are connected with the balance of power between different factions within the union, the structure of the union, the degree to which it controls entry to employment, the degree of competition between unions, and so on. However, since the determinants of the union's policy will be a set of internal decisions made in the light of all these factors, we may call the indifference curve of the union the 'internal trade-off' between wages and employment. As we shall see shortly, the union will maximise utility by equating the slope of its internal trade-off with the slope of the labour demand curve.

The nature of the trade-off

Whilst we shall conduct our analysis on the assumption that the union's utility function may be reduced to the two arguments, wages and employment, we must recognise that in reality this assumption obscures many complex issues. Even without straying into the very intricate area of industrial relations matters that are of crucial importance to trade unions, there are many economic matters effectively subsumed under the wage/employment trade-off which we take to be the utility function of the union.

When we talk of 'wages' in the context of the trade-off we are in fact referring to a whole range of different aspects of pay. The term 'wages' includes such things as overtime, shift and other premia; it also includes pensions, holiday and sick pay and special pay arrangements for periods when workers are laid off for one reason and another. Piecework pay raises its own problems but is included in the category of wages, as are redundancy payments, fringe benefits, and so on. Accordingly one is tempted to query whether 'wages' is an adequate generic term on which to base our analysis. The answer really has to be affirmative since the analysis would become unmanageable if every aspect of wages were to be treated individually, but also because both union and employer may well view the individual elements of wages as close substitutes for each other and therefore as being parts of the same *economic* package. In other words, it may not matter much to employers which element of their labour costs (total gross pay) the union seeks to increase since the net effect will be to increase their labour costs per unit of labour and *that* is the key variable. Similarly, unions may be content simply to increase gross wages for their members by achieving increases in any component part. While this is sufficient, for analytical purposes, to allow us to view wages as a single package of payments, it is not strictly correct. Neither unions nor employers will in practice regard all of the components of pay as *perfect* substitutes — improved redundancy pay in a declining industry is not a perfect substitute for improved basic pay, for example — but the main implications of this are that employer and union tactics about the wage 'package' will vary according to the needs of particular situations while their general economic effects remain rather similar.

The other argument in the utility function which we have used to describe union preferences is 'employment' but, unlike 'wages', this is a fairly straightforward concept. In this context employment must be taken to mean the number of persons employed. Phenomena such as overtime working and short-time working may reasonably be subsumed under the term employment but the general meaning of the term in our analysis is otherwise unambiguous.

There is an important sense in which we ought to further consider the meaning of employment in the context of the trade-off with wages. In a perfectly competitive labour market the trade-off between jobs and wages would be a straightforward mechanical one subject to considerations of profit maximisation. In practice however, unions have established a measure of control in respect of the rules which govern certain aspects of employment and these limit the freedom of employers to hire and fire in response to changes in wage rates. Hence, unions have established rules which govern the allocation of work (manning schedules for example), restrictions on entry to the employment (apprenticeship rules for example), lay-off procedures (last in/first out for example) and various employment security provisions (tenure or established jobs for example). These rules of employment make marginal adjustments in the numbers employed difficult for employers to effect and thereby blunt the sharpness of the trade-off in the short run.

Further, there has been a trend in recent years towards higher monetary compensation for individuals who are laid off. This has been achieved in two ways and has been vigorously promoted by trade unions. First, lump-sum payments of various kinds are now common when a worker loses his job. Severance pay, redundancy payments and lump-sum inducements to workers to quit voluntarily are examples and are common in the industrial countries. In some cases these payments are voluntary but in others are the subject of legislation. Second, unemployment compensation has tended to rise to historically high levels relative to average earnings. (See chapter 11.) The effects of both of these trends has been to reduce the cost to the individual of losing his job and presumably has led trade unions to place a lower weight on marginal job losses than they would have done some years ago and to increase the costs to employers of laying off labour. Hence, to the extent that the unions have been able to reduce the costs of member unemployment in these ways, and to the extent that they are able to further reduce it in the future, union policy on this front will be reflected in favourable changes in the trade-off between wages and employment.

Neither the unions' policies on direct control over employment nor in respect of reducing the costs of member unemployment fall within the meaning of 'employment' when we talk of a trade-off between wages and unemployment. Instead they are policies which are designed to alter the shape of the indifference curves in their utility map by altering the sensitivity of the employment argument in relation to wages in the wage/employment trade-off.

The concept of union labour supply and the wage preference path

We have arrived at a concept of union labour supply based on the idea that the union will conceive of its utility function as a trade-off between wages and employment. Higher wages can only be obtained by sacrificing some employment, and higher employment only by sacrificing some (potential) wage increase, so long as the demand for labour is fixed and negatively sloped. Hence the *cost* of higher wages is lower employment and the *cost* of higher employment is a lower (potential) wage increase. We arrived at this concept simply by considering the economic implications for a union of providing improved economic utility for a group of workers who were not unionised before. Now our concept is a simple one and we can develop it further. Before this, however, let us consider for a moment the way in which the union has been treated in economic theory in the past.

The union as a one-variable maximiser

Until the early 1950s there was a tendency in economics to view unions as economic agents analogous to firms. This was natural since the neo-classical theory of the firm was a well-established and convenient analytical framework of analysis and, if the union could be assumed to behave in a manner analogous to the firm, it could easily be absorbed into that framework. The characteristic of the firm which had also 'to be attributed to the union in order to establish the analogy was that it sought to maximise a single variable — profits in the case of the firm. Hence various efforts were made to discover some single variable which it could reasonably be assumed that trade unions wished to maximise.

Wages or employment

Now there are some assumptions which we may dispose of without further ado. Suppose the union was assumed to maximise the wage rate. Where the demand for labour is given and is a negatively-sloped function this implies that the union would seek the highest possible wage rate for the smallest feasible workgroup and therefore trade almost all its members' jobs in the process. That cannot be right. In the extreme case the union would be left with only one member earning a huge wage. Similarly if the union is conceived of as an employment maximiser, it will end up with a large employed membership at the market wage and there will be no utility gains to any previously employed member. Hence the union cannot be assumed to maximise either the wage rate or employment only.

The wage bill

It has occasionally been suggested that it is reasonable to view the union as attempting to maximise the wage bill accruing to its members, i.e. the wage multiplied by the numbers employed. This is equivalent to the case of the monopolist with zero marginal costs who maximises profit by fixing price and quantity at the point of unitary elasticity on the demand curve. (Cournot's case of the owner of a mineral spring is the classic example of this.) This case is illustrated in fig. 3.4. Here we do not explicitly introduce a labour supply curve since we are here viewing the union simply as an agent operating (costlessly) on behalf of its members to locate a *point* on the demand curve at which a perfectly elastic short-run supply of union labour can be offered. The wage bill is maximised at point Z which yields a wage of W_1 and employment of L_1. Point Z on the demand curve for labour is the point at which the elasticity of demand is unity.

There are a number of objections to this view of trade union policy. The first is practical. It would be extremely difficult for the union to know when it was maximising the wage bill even if it were able to experiment on a significant scale. Secondly, the trade-off between wages and employment implied by such a policy would be uniquely determined by a single objective and this runs counter to all that we have said about the balance which unions must strike between different interests within themselves. Thirdly, since the elasticity of labour demand differs widely between and within employments, a structure of union wage rates would emerge which varied so widely that competition *amongst union labour* would ensue and would make the maintenance of such a policy

Fig. 3.4

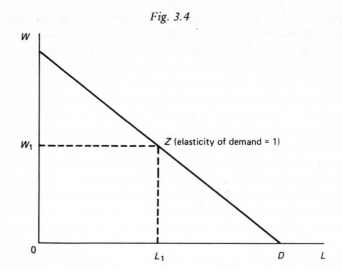

virtually impossible. Any casual observation demonstrates that uniform rather than varied union wage rates tend to be the rule for homogeneous groups of labour (see Flanagan, 1976).

While we must therefore dismiss the possibility that unions are in fact attempting to be wage bill maximisers, it is worth noting that in welfare terms this would be the optimum economic policy to pursue so long as total wages could be pooled and each worker paid an equal share of the pool.

The wage membership function

Dunlop has suggested that unions may be conceived of as attempting to maximise their membership. His analysis holds that the number of employees who will attach themselves to a union is a function of the union wage rate. Hence he suggests the concept of a 'wage membership function' as a union labour supply function. This is illustrated in fig. 3.5.

WMF is the wage membership function and indicates the numbers of employees who will be union members at any given wage rate. For example, at point X the wage membership function equates with the demand for labour and the wage rate is OW_u and employment and union membership will be OL_u. If the union were to seek to maximise employment by fixing the wage at its competitive level OW_n then employment would increase to OL_n but union membership would fall by $L_1 L_u$. Clearly in the case of a closed or union shop (where union membership is required in order to work) the 'market' supply curve and the wage membership function would coincide.

This approach lacks credibility on a number of grounds. First, while it is certainly true that unions have an instinctive desire to maximise their

membership, it is very difficult to believe that this can be their primary object.*
Secondly, it is unrealistic to suppose that the level of the union wage is the
prime determinant of the extent of union membership. No doubt the economic
success of a union does influence the numbers who join it but economic success
can be gauged in terms of more variables than simply the union wage. Hence,
even if membership were the maximand, common sense tells us that the demand
for union services is a function of variables which are not strictly economic —
such as access to grievance procedures, union representation in disputes over
non-economic issues and protection against arbitrary management decisions — as
well as of economic variables. Thirdly, as we have noted, a union is unlikely to
regard the aggregate of its membership as homogeneous. If Ross is anywhere
near the mark, unions will recognise that their membership is heterogeneous and
that the particular aspirations of different elements within it have to be specially
catered for. This is inconsistent with the simple membership-maximising model.
Finally, even if increasing its membership is central to union policy it may well
be that the net returns to recruitment equate with the marginal costs of
organising at levels of unionisation below the maximum. Hence it may be
economically irrational for a union to attempt to maximise its membership. This
sort of situation may arise, for example, in unionising unskilled female labour.
Such labour is difficult and costly to organise and often yields low returns to the
union because the membership tends to be unstable.

In defence of Dunlop it should be said that various unions at various
times — the CIO unions in the USA during the 1930s and the general unions in
Britain almost since their inception — have given the outward impression that

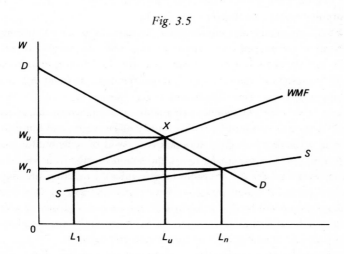

Fig. 3.5

---

*Moreover, it is implied that the union is unconcerned with its unemployed members.

growth of membership was their central objective. However, the reasons for this and the methods employed are not entirely consistent with the concept of the wage membership function. The primary motivation for rapid and extensive recruitment has usually resulted from the need to establish a sufficiently large base in an industry to prevent the substitution of non-union for union labour – which is not the same as maximising membership – and the methods employed, though varied, have mainly involved direct appeals to workers, based on the promise that the union would protect them against exploitation and the worst abuses of factory life, and influencing governments to make it difficult to remain outside the union.

The wage preference path

A rather more sophisticated approach to the construction of a union labour supply function has been developed in recent years and we outline it in some detail below.

We take as our starting point the concept which we encountered earlier of the internal trade-off between wages and employment as the expression of the union's utility function. Hence we represent the union as operating in accordance with a map of indifference curves relating combinations of wages and employment which manifest the union's tastes and preferences. Now for any given demand curve for labour the union's utility function is maximised at the point at which the slope of an indifference curve is equal to the slope of the demand curve. Thus, a variety of utility-maximising positions may be identified within the union's indifference map by reference to *a series of different potential demand curves*. This is a quasi-dynamic element in our concept of the union labour supply curve and is illustrated in fig. 3.6.

The figure illustrates four indifference curves in the union's indifference map at the point in time when the current wage is OW_2 and employment is OL_2, i.e. when the current utility-maximising position is indicated by the point of tangency between a demand curve and indifference curve at X_2. From the vantage point of the current situation the union projects its preferences through higher and lower levels of labour demand by tracing out the expansion path linking all points of tangency between indifference curves and demand curves. Hence at *a moment of time* the union is conceived of as formulating a supply function of labour in respect of all possible demand curves for labour which can only refer *to other points in time*. So long as we view the wage preference path as a supply curve of union labour, it is not difficult to employ it as a tool of analysis in comparative statics. We simply need to analyse discrete movements from one equilibrium situation to another by isolating the relevant segment of the wage preference path. Collective bargaining and the relative bargaining power of the two sides will determine the exact location of actual wage/employment combinations as demand changes. Now this is a different concept from that of a market labour supply function where wage/employment combinations below the

Fig. 3.6

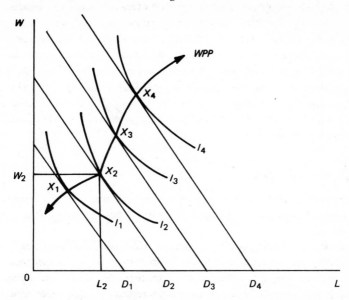

supply curve are not feasible since the desired number of workers will simply not supply their labour at wage rates below the supply curve.

The complexities of this approach to union labour supply make general analysis of the wage determination process, by means of comparative statics and conventional neo-classical assumptions, more difficult. The main problems stem from the indeterminate nature of the union supply curve (*ex post*), the quasi-dynamic model which is implied in this approach and the need to specify the determinants of 'relative bargaining power' as the final arbiter of wage determination. While we describe these as 'complexities' we do not do so in a critical manner. It has long been felt that the simple framework of neo-classical microeconomics is not a suitable analytical framework within which to study wage determination under trade unionism. These 'complexities' are largely an injection of realistic assumptions about the economic role of unions into the otherwise conventional neo-classical framework. Let us proceed to the final stage of our treatment of union labour supply before drawing conclusions.

The union wage preference path is likely to be asymmetrical around the current wage/employment situation, i.e. unions will not respond to falls in labour demand in the same way as they will to increases. This proposition is illustrated in fig. 3.7.

The wage preference path is kinked around the current situation at X in such a way as to indicate that unions will vigorously resist wage reductions and trade away employment to do so when demand falls, whereas when demand rises they will tend to divide the demand increases more equally between wage increases

Fig. 3.7

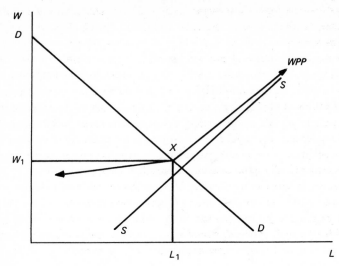

and employment growth. This assumption accords with experience and is also in accord with an important empirical finding, reported by Lewis (1963a), that in the USA the desired differential between union and non-union wages, which is indicated for any given level of demand by the vertical distance between the *WPP* and the market supply curve *SS*, tends to be highest when demand for labour generally is low, and lowest when demand for labour is high. This can be explained by the rigidity of union wages in times of rising demand and by shifts in the relative importance of individual, as opposed to collective, bargaining power. These are matters to which we shall return in detail in chapter 6.

Now this model is explicitly indeterminate about the supply of union labour which will be offered at any given wage since relative bargaining power will determine the actual locus of settlements which are negotiated. Hence all that we can know from the concept of the wage preference path is that *at a point in time* the employer and the union will agree to a wage/employment combination which is reasonably close to the utility-maximising solution for both (closer to the utility-maximising solution of the party with the greater bargaining power), and that the union will supply labour in a perfectly elastic manner at the agreed wage.

The element of indeterminacy in the model is of some importance since it permits us to analyse the process of collective bargaining in a systematic way. Indeed any model of union wage policy which is always *determinate* relegates the process of collective bargaining to the status of an empty ritual or implicitly assumes that one or other party can always impose its will on the other. The only important exception is the neo-classical bilateral monopoly model (see chapter 7) in which, using conventional analysis but assuming that collective bargaining is characterised by a monopolist (the union) and a monopsonist (the employers' association) confronting each other, a range of indeterminacy is explicit (see Zeuthen, 1930). The idea that a union can be looked at by analogy to a business monopoly is an old one in economics. There are some problems in this analogy: the classical monopolist may forgo output in order to maximise profits (which is costless) but the union must forgo employment for its members in order to maximise utility, and that involves costs; in many cases the union has little real idea of the actual employment costs of any increase in wages and is normally unable to recontract in order to correct misjudgments, while the product market monopolist is probably more aware of economic realities and can recontract to correct misjudgments; and unions typically operate in situations closer to oligopoly or competition than pure monopoly.

Our model is sufficiently flexible to incorporate the main elements of any monopolistic characteristics of union behaviour and at the same time provide us with a more general and realistic model than the simple monopoly analogy alone can provide. We shall proceed, therefore, to analyse the economic behaviour of unions, assuming that they behave approximately as our model predicts.

Conventional criteria in union wage policy

At a more practical level we should note that unions often appear to pursue wage policies based on rules of thumb. (We ignore inter-union wage relationships here since they are dealt with in detail in the next chapter.) For example, it has been argued that unions will pursue some target rate of growth of the real wage over the long run (e.g. Johnson and Timbrell, 1974). This notion is based on the idea that unions have become accustomed, over a long period of time, to a rate of growth of real wages approximately equal to the rate of growth of real output and that they become conditioned to aim at securing this historical rate of growth of real wages. Where short-run factors make it impossible to secure their target in any period, unions will seek appropriately larger wage increases in subsequent periods in order to 'catch up'.

It is true that, for example in Britain, real wages have tended to rise over the post-war period at around 2% over the long period and that that is about the same as the trend rate of increase of real output per man. Moreover, experience of the periods which immediately follow the relaxation or abandonment of incomes policies does suggest that unions attempt to 'catch up' on deviations from the trend. Is this inconsistent with the model of union wage policy outlined in the rest of this chapter? The answer is, of course, no. If unions choose to pursue a policy of stable growth of real wages over the long period, this simply implies that they have adopted a particular *WPP* in which a particular wage target is the dominant feature and the employment implications are accepted as the cost of the wage policy.

A policy of ensuring that the growth of the union real wage is on average in line with the trend growth rate of real output per man is an economically sensible one in the context of an economy which is successfully pursuing 'full-employment' policies. However, in the context of relatively high unemployment – such as existed in almost all industrial countries after 1970 – the employment costs of following a fixed real wage growth policy become important, particularly if productivity growth slows down also. Unions are therefore generally prepared to modify their wage policy in such circumstances – as they have done under the Wage-Price Guideposts system in the USA and various Prices and Incomes Policies in Britain – and this represents a shift in the utility weight accorded to the employment objective. If ground lost in this process can be recovered at a later stage, when employment costs become less important, a 'catch-up' policy is quite appropriate.

Various other rules of thumb have been suggested as criteria for union wage policy. For example, it has been variously argued that unions tailor their wage policy to secure wage targets *net* of tax and social security payments (Flemming, 1976), to emulate union achievements in other countries (Wiles, 1973) or in response to feelings of 'relative deprivation' (Baxter, 1973). It is important to be clear that these are not, in themselves, complete theories of union wage policy but are instead the inputs which determine the final shape of the particular wage policy which is pursued. Hence they describe the general considerations which lead to the adoption of any particular wage policy, in terms only of the wage objective – they do not take account of the constraints imposed by the non-wage arguments in the union's utility function which determine the precise form of its wage policy. Hence our concept of union wage policy being formulated by a trade-off between wage and employment (and other) variables is sufficiently elastic to accommodate these more specific interpretations of why this or that union followed some particular wage policy at some point in time.

Closed versus open unionism

It is useful at this stage to make a distinction, in terms of wage policy, between closed and open unions. It is particularly appropriate to do so here since we are able to cross-check independent hypotheses about this distinction against a reasonable inference of the model developed in this chapter.

It has variously been proposed (e.g. Friedman, 1951) that the effective supply curve of craft union labour will differ from that of the industrial or general union. The two conventional situations are illustrated in fig. 3.8.

Inspection of fig. 3.8 reveals that closed unions appear to place a greater weight on wages relative to employment, both when demand falls and when it rises, than do open unions. There are a number of reasons for this – some of the more important ones involve the *ability* to do so – but consider those which involve only union preferences in the context of our general model. Characteristics of the closed union are that it comprises workers who possess skills for which there is normally no substitute in the short run, that its members are

Fig. 3.8

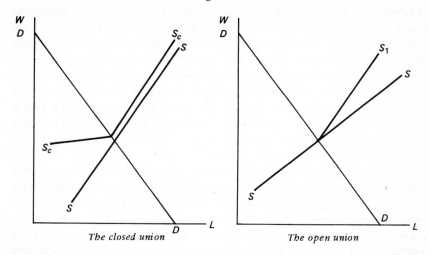

The closed union

The open union

usually admitted on the basis of a selection process operating through controls on entry to the facilities needed to acquire the approved skills and through entry charges, and the union is often run like an exclusive club. These are some of the ingredients of the 'job-rationing' function associated with craft unions (see Perlman, 1928). Now in these circumstances the craft union will be prepared to trade employment in order to maintain the wage rate, since it will regard any such losses of employment as phenomena which will not last long — because the same men who are made unemployed will be re-employed when demand increases — and since it will often have (or government may have) made arrangements which very effectively cushion the cost of unemployment to the individuals involved. (For example, special lay-off arrangements may have been negotiated, earnings-related unemployment compensation may be provided and rehiring rules may exist.) Similarly, in keeping with the job-rationing ethic which is designed to prevent labour surpluses emerging, closed unions will tend to put the emphasis on increased wages rather than increased employment when demand rises. Also, closed union members often tend to be highly mobile between industries so that the supply curve facing any particular industry or firm will tend to be highly elastic when demand falls but highly inelastic when demand is rising. More specifically, the transfer earnings of any closed union member in relation to a particular firm or industry are likely to be about the same as their current wage. For these reasons it is important to note that the effective bargaining unit for a closed union is rarely coextensive with the employments of its members, and this contrasts with the situation of the industrial union where the bargaining unit is normally the industry itself.

Open unions cannot exercise the same degree of control over entry to employment as do closed unions. Their members are heterogeneous in skills — many having no skills at all — and substitute labour (not necessarily non-union but from other unions as well) is normally available. In a situation of this kind it is virtually impossible to control entry effectively to the industry unless the industry is coextensive with an occupation or group of occupations linked by a craft union or coalition of craft unions, e.g. as in the printing industry. The economic implications of this for open unions are that their optimal strategy will be to try to prevent large employment losses occurring when demand falls, by trading away some of the current wage; otherwise the unions could be ruined by a sustained loss of members which might turn out to be permanent, or at least so prolonged that the unions might find it extremely hard to recover. Fortunately, from the point of view of the economist, there is an example of an open union which chose to place an extremely high relative weight on wages in the face of declining demand, and it is instructive to note that the union concerned, the United Mine Workers of America, which forced wages up rapidly during the 1920s, almost went out of existence because of the resulting loss of members.

In situations of rising demand it is less clear that the policy of a closed union will attach any greater weight to increased wages than an open union, although the restrictionist ethic underlying the closed union's policy, taken together with the general impression that open unions attach considerable importance to the sheer volume of their membership, suggests that it may well be that closed unions pursue a more wage-conscious policy than open unions.

This description of the difference between the policies of closed unions on the one hand and open unions on the other is basically derived from observation of what they actually do. (Friedman, 1951, has, for example, made a distinction largely based on empirical observation.) The important point, however, is that, by using the analytical framework of our general model, we could have *predicted* such description without the aid of any actual observations other than of the main characteristics of the two types of unions. Now this in no way 'validates' our model, but it is helpful to know at this stage that the model is consistent with the facts of one particular situation which can be cross-checked and this lends some credibility to it.

Summary

We began this chapter by briefly discussing the neo-classical analysis of labour supply and observed that it views the individual's utility function as a trade-off between income and leisure. Proceeding from this model to a model of workgroup utility functions readily suggests that what is true for the individual will, of course, be true for the group so long as we allow for differences in people's tastes and preferences. Now, in the absence of unions, both of these situations are characterised by a fixed wage, and therefore variations in hours supplied are the only means of adjustment. When a union is introduced into the group to act as the agent charged with maximising group utility, we observed that the union can only increase the utility of its members over that which existed before unionisation by increasing the wage rate.

The union therefore adopts a utility function which it perceives to have two arguments — employment and wages — *both* of which are in principle variable. Since the services of a union will only be demanded and retained when it is securing a higher level of utility for its members than they would secure for themselves in its absence, the union must set about raising the wage rate above its competitive level. However, the union faces the same sort of trade-off as the individual faced, although for the union it is a trade-off between wages and employment rather than one between income and leisure. (This is an oversimplification since unions will also trade hours for wages in certain situations, e.g. where worksharing is adopted by the union as an alternative to lay-offs.)

At a point in time the maximisation of the union's utility function is achieved by equating the marginal rate of substitution between wages and employment on an indifference curve (the slope of the indifference curve) with the slope of the labour demand curve. We have proposed a model which allows us to cast the analysis in quasi-dynamic form by tracing out the expansion path — which is the locus of all utility-maximising combinations of wages and employment for all higher and lower levels of demand than the current one — through the utility map of the union. This device specifically provides for indeterminacy in wage fixing and therefore gives us a method of analysing the collective bargaining process.

This model is probably the most satisfactory economic 'maximising' model and, while it is a highly simplified construct, provides a basis for the economic analysis of union wage determination. It is, for example, a useful tool in analysing the conventional distinction made between the wage policy of closed unions and that of open unions.

Further reading

A. M. Cartter *Theory of Wages and Employment* Illinois, Irwin (1959).
A. M. Ross *Trade Union Wage Policy* Berkeley, University of California Press (1948).
J. T. Dunlop *Wage Determination under Trade Unions* New York, Kelley (1950).

CHAPTER 4

The Interaction of Union Wage Policies

In the previous chapter we implicitly dealt with an individual trade union's wage policy as though that policy was independent of the policies of other unions. In this chapter we shall briefly consider how trade union wage policies may be interrelated with each other and examine the implications of this for our simple model. In this sense the chapter is an extension of the previous one, designed to highlight a particularly important special aspect of union wage policy.

The general issues

It is conventionally accepted that most trade unions formulate their wage policy with an eye to the wage policy they expect or observe other unions to follow. This is a matter on which both Ross and Dunlop were agreed and there is a considerable literature on the topic (also see Flanagan, 1976, for an empirical study).

There are many reasons why unions will formulate their own wage policy in relation to the policies of other unions, some of these reasons being purely economic and others quasi-political. An example of an economic reason is when two unions organise similar labour, or the members of one union are good substitutes for the members of the other. In such a case, if one union negotiated a lower wage than the other, the latter would find its members being displaced in employment by members of the 'low wage' union. (It would of course depend on the ability of employers to substitute the members of one union for those of another.) It may be objected that the wage/employment trade-off of each union will already reflect this possibility. This, however, is not so in an atomised collective bargaining environment since unions vary in power, employers vary in their resistance to unions' wage demands and a number of circumstantial variables can affect the outcome of the bargaining process. Hence we are in a situation rather like that of product market oligopoly where discontinuities in individual demand curves exist as a result of uncertainty about the pricing policy of competitors. Indeed it is often more appropriate to apply to unions the analogy of the oligopolist in the product market than that of the monopolist.

An example of a political reason for a union to relate its wage policy to that of other unions is the case in which some conventional (but not economically determined) relation between the wages of two unions has been established. Any deviation from the conventional wage relation – however desirable from an economic point of view – may be interpreted as a failure on the part of a union's leadership and may drive them into taking apparently irrational actions to restore the relationship. Ross cites the example of a union leader prepared to plunge his union into a costly strike when the union is being offered only a cent less than the settlement it desires. Economically such an action may make no sense (leaving aside for the moment the need to maintain the credibility of strike threats) but it may be politically imperative if the extra cent is required to obtain the wage already achieved by some other union with which a conventional wage relation exists or which is a direct competitor for members.

Now the importance of this for our analysis is that the actual determination of the union wage in any particular case may be significantly influenced by the outcome of other unions' wage negotiations; this would result in a certain rigidity in the structure of relative union wages and explain the phenomenon known as 'pattern bargaining' in the USA and the 'wage transfer mechanism' in Britain. Note at this stage that these phenomena may often be explicable in purely economic terms – i.e. they may be market determined – and that we are confining ourselves to a discussion of those which are politically or institutionally determined (see Addison and Burton, 1977, on this distinction).

Conventional relationships between union wages

Over long periods of time the collective bargaining system of most countries throws up sets of conventions which serve to establish customary links between the wages of different groups of union workers. In some instances these links exist within unions, most notably in industrial unions, but the more important cases are where the links are between unions or between bargaining units.

There are two basic types of link. First there is 'horizontal equity'. This forms a link between the wages of workers of approximately the same level of skill – e.g. bus drivers and truck drivers – and typically tends to be manifested in a common rate of pay extending throughout all the employments in which the two groups of workers are found. Ross has called this phenomenon 'orbits of coercive comparison' and Dunlop talks of 'wage contours', while the term 'comparability' is most frequently used in Britain. In Sweden the central trade union congress, the LO, has explicitly endorsed horizontal equity as a principle of pay policy. The second link is called 'vertical equity' and forms a conventional link between the pay of one skill group and that of another group possessing greater or less skill. This results in conventional wage 'differentials' between different groups of labour – e.g. between bus driver and bus conductor – and these differentials are found both within particular employments and across employments. They are part of the system of 'orbits of coercive comparison' and the map of 'wage contours'.

Both horizontal and vertical equity tend to be central criteria in wage bargaining, mainly on the union side but often on the employer side too, since it is often less costly to be a price-taker than a price-maker. Depending on how deeply they are entrenched they are important sources of relative wage rigidity and consequently have implications for the allocation of labour and for the process of wage inflation.

Collective bargaining in Britain and the USA is riddled with practices rooted in custom and convention and it is often not known how or why they arose. In continental Europe such practices are less evident and where they do exist they are normally traceable to some social objective of the trade unions involved.

Horizontal equity

In general the criterion of horizontal equity — under such slogans as 'equal pay for equal work' — appears to have been adopted by trade unions in order to protect the wages of the weakest elements in their membership against market forces by linking their wages to those of the strongest groups, and to limit the degree of competition amongst union labour.* This is a reflection of the social and political consciousness of many trade unions and has its public policy parallel in statutory minimum wage rates such as are applied in the USA. Moreover, where collective bargaining is of a centralised kind — where a single bargaining unit determines wages throughout a large segment of the labour force — it is both convenient and often politically imperative to negotiate common rates for similar types of labour irrespective of the industry or area in which they are employed.

Another reason why horizontal equity is so pervasive a force in collective bargaining is that many employers — particularly small and unimportant ones — do not engage in direct collective bargaining over wages. The costs of doing so may be quite high and such employers often prefer simply to allow for an automatic link between the wages of their employees and those of some outside group. This amounts to an automatic formula for wage adjustments which saves the union and the employer the costs and trouble of direct negotiation.

H. A. Turner (1957) provides an engrossing account of the role of horizontal and vertical equity in the development of the British wage structure and the tenacity with which they are maintained. He cites the case of the wages of policemen and firemen in Britain. Their wages were linked continuously over the 30 years from 1920 to 1950, despite the major economic upheavals which occurred during that period, and the link was only finally broken in 1951 because of a persistent shortage of policemen. When the pay of policemen was

---

*This may of course result in lower employment amongst the 'weakest' groups than if their wages were determined independently.

raised, the firemen attempted to keep in line with them but were refused and the result was a major and prolonged industrial dispute. In another article Turner (1952) gives examples of cases in which horizontal equity linked the pay of different groups of workers for up to 60 years.

Vertical equity

Like horizontal equity, the conventional or customary relationships between the pay of one grade of labour and another – the 'differential' – has an obscure history. In all probability the concept of an appropriate differential has its origins in the period when only craft unionism existed and the wages of skilled craftsmen and apprentices were related by some fixed formula. The coming of mass unionism, which drew unskilled workers into unions, appears to have extended the concept of the established differential by relating the unskilled workers' wage to that of apprentices. The absorption of vast numbers of semi-skilled workers into unions with the growth of mass production industries did not, however, simply extend the system of established differentials but rather encouraged the emergence of a more diverse system of collective bargaining than the straightforward national agreement.

Although the extent of the system of vertical equity was not increased by the inclusion of semi-skilled workers in unions, it remains a pervasive force in union wage structures throughout Europe and North America. The differential is sometimes measured as a percentage wage difference and sometimes as a flat rate sum of money, but the stability of both types of differential has been quite remarkable over the whole of this century.

Union wage policy about wage differentials will clearly vary according to the type of union concerned, the economic environment and the internal political balance of the union. In a general way closed unions appear to have conceived of their 'appropriate' differential over other workers in percentage terms and have normally been content to maintain the differential in the face of egalitarian wage policies pursued by other unions and sometimes by governments. Open unions, on the other hand, have had to strike a balance between the various occupations within their membership in formulating a policy on wage differentials between them.

Now there are some economic issues which we must clarify before proceeding. In the first place there will always be some set of optimal wage differentials, which will be determined by the forces of supply and demand for different types of labour. In turn, such differentials, taken together with the costs of acquiring education and training, will determine the rates of return on investment in various types of skill or 'human capital'. In a perfectly competitive market, therefore, there will be a unique set of wage differentials between different types of workers which will ensure that the labour market is cleared. Where trade union activity has the effect of distorting the structure of differentials which would exist in the competitive context, then shortages of certain types of labour and surpluses of other types will emerge. The market will not then be cleared and 'structural unemployment' will exist in the short run (see Rees, 1951).

Now, just as we recognised that trade union activity is unlikely simply to rubber-stamp the wage rate which a competitive market would have produced, we cannot assume that the structure of relative union wages will be the same as that which a competitive market would have produced. An important implication of this is, of course, that labour will be deployed inefficiently. We return to this matter in chapter 10, but for the moment we concentrate on the concept of vertical equity as an aspect of union wage policy, and some of its implications for union behaviour.

The criterion of vertical equity is often an attractive one for unions and employers, and sometimes for governments. It provides convenient rules of thumb for determining the relationships which ought to exist between different groups of workers, it frequently carries an aura of 'fairness' about it and it is an effective method of protecting the wages (but not the employment) of economically weak groups of workers. It is often wholly institutionalised within such arrangements as job-evaluation systems for these very reasons (particularly in 'internal labour markets' – see Doeringer and Piore, 1971. For these reasons – and also because long-standing conventions often become sacred cows in trade union affairs – vertical equity has become an entrenched feature of union wage policy. However, the criterion of vertical equity has had to contend with two important trends which have progressively undermined its viability.

First we noted that in some cases vertical equity is expressed in wage differentials measured in money rather than percentages. Since the Second World War wage inflation has eroded the percentage differential where that differential is measured in money terms. In addition there has been a perceptible trend towards a narrowing of wage differentials in both Britain and the USA due to a variety of factors including union and government inspired policies aimed at improving the relative position of the lower-paid workers (see Turner, 1957).

This latter factor is particularly important in the case of skilled members of open unions, where the bulk of the membership is unskilled or semi-skilled and where the union must therefore pay particular attention to the interests of those groups. In this situation skilled workers will observe the erosion of their differential and frequently resort to drastic action to remedy the perceived injustice. For example, the United Automobile Workers in the USA have often had to negotiate special agreements on behalf of their skilled members in order to head off attempts by these workers to break away from the UAW and set up their own union. Similarly in Britain a major dispute in British Leyland occurred in early 1977 when toolroom workers (unsuccessfully) demanded negotiations with the management separate from those covering production workers.

All these pressures become more intense when government-imposed incomes policies or wage/price guidelines are in force and permit only flat-rate money adjustments in wages for all. In continental Europe, percentage differentials predominate in the system of vertical equity and this particular strain on the system is less acute.

The second trend is an economic one. In any dynamic economy the structure of demand for labour will be continuously changing and, if the structure of labour supply is to change appropriately, then there must be some flexibility in the structure of relative wages. Rigid application of criteria of vertical equity prevents such flexibility and can lead to shortages of particular groups of labour. For example, a rise in the demand for skilled craftsmen may occur but the differential between the wages of skilled craftsmen and semi- or unskilled labour may be insufficient to encourage workers to invest in the required skills; this will lead to a shortage of skilled labour. Rees (1951) shows how problems of this kind arose in the US steel industry.

Relative wage rigidity

Taken together, the effects of the criteria of horizontal and vertical equity on the wage structure are to make relative wages inflexible or rigid. Hence there is a case for believing that unions may create a rigid structure of wages independent of any wage gains which they secure over the market wage. This is a matter which is discussed in general by Keynes (1936) and which has implications for wage inflation and for the allocation of resources in the economy.

The main inflationary implications of relative wage rigidity are that when *any* wage rate is increased – i.e. the wage of any significant group of workers – there will be a tendency to generalise that increase through the chain reaction of increases brought about by the application of the criteria of vertical and horizontal equity. Hence one group of workers may experience a sharp increase in the demand for their services while there is no increase in the demand for labour in general. However, the increase in the wages of the 'key group' may be generalised through a series of claims for increases by other workers, supported only by reference to conventional relativities between the wages of different groups. Evidence that such a process may be a systematic feature of wage inflation is afforded by the post-war experience of the Irish Republic where certain skilled crafts have consistently been in excess demand and have pulled the whole wage level up year after year as a result of the power of the system of wage relativities in that country (see C. Mulvey and J. A. Trevithick, 1974). A more sophisticated Keynesian approach to relative wage rigidities and wage inflation is to be found in Trevithick (1976). (See Jackson *et al.*, 1972, for evidence on Britain, and Addison and Burton, 1977, for a survey of US evidence.)

So far as the question of the allocation of resources is concerned, union-induced relative wage rigidity will clearly reduce labour mobility by stifling the allocative function of relative wages. Hence we would expect a sub-optimal allocation of resources to result and this, along with other welfare aspects of trade union activity, is discussed in chapter 10.

Other aspects of union wage interaction

We have concentrated on the general issues of horizontal and vertical equity as vehicles for union wage interactions. Similar wage interactions are often encountered in other, more particular, situations. For example, a conventional relation may exist between union wages in different geographical areas, between the sexes, between racial groups or between age groups. The implications of such conventional relations are the same as for the general cases of horizontal and vertical equity. In general, unions have pursued egalitarian policies about these differentials, and this has raised problems of the kind discussed above.

Summary

While we are mainly concerned with the effects of unions on the wages of their members relative to those who are not in unions and on the overall effects which unions may have on the wage level, it is important to be aware that union wages themselves may interact with each other and that this has economic implications. The union wage interaction may be a straightforward economic phenomenon but more often tends to be a product of custom and convention based on conceptions of 'equity' between different groups of workers.

The main links between union wages tend to be between the wages of comparable occupational groups – 'horizontal equity' – and between the wages of hierarchies of different occupational groups – 'vertical equity'. Other conventional relationships exist for male/female wages, geographical groups and racial groups. The main effects of this phenomenon are to make the structure of relative wages inflexible and this will tend to have inflationary consequences and to distort the allocation of resources in the economy.

Unions themselves experience a variety of problems arising from such wage interactions. General union policies which are egalitarian tend – especially in open unions – to raise difficulties with the skilled workers in their membership. This introduces an element of conflict into union policy formulation – a matter extensively dealt with by Arthur Ross (1948). All of this should be seen primarily as an added dimension of union wage policy formulation, the main lines of which were discussed in chapter 3. However, the economic implications of these issues have particular significance in certain areas of analysis, and so we shall return to them from time to time in later chapters.

Finally, an extensive and illuminating set of examples of the manner in which these wage interactions occur in practice – drawn from British experience – is to be found in Turner (1957).

Further reading

A. M. Ross *Trade Union Wage Policy* Berkeley, University of California Press (1948).

R. J. Flanagan, 'Wage interdependence in unionised labor markets' *Brookings Papers on Economic Activity* (1976, 3).

H. A. Turner 'Inflation and wage differentials in Great Britain' in J. T. Dunlop (ed.) *The Theory of Wage Determination* London, Macmillan (1957).

H. A. Turner 'Trade union organisation' *Political Quarterly* (1955) and reprinted in B. J. McCormick and E. O. Smith (eds) *The Labour Market* Penguin Books (1968).

J. T. Dunlop 'The wage structure: job clusters and wage contours' in G. W. Taylor (ed.) *New Concepts in Wage Determination* New York, McGraw-Hill (1957).

CHAPTER 5

Unions and the Demand for Labour

In the previous two chapters we have outlined a framework of trade union wage policy which provides us with a basis for analysing the supply of labour in unionised labour markets. In this chapter we shall explore some issues relating to the demand for labour which are relevant to the analysis of wage determination under trade unions.

In a perfectly competitive world – that is, where 'pure competition' reigned in all markets – there would be no net economic advantage to society in the existence of trade unions. Welfare gains to union members deriving from union activity would be offset by welfare losses to the community as a whole. However, we do not live in such a world, and imperfections in both product and labour markets dominate the capitalist economies. Such imperfections imply the existence of a net welfare loss to the community, with welfare gains and losses to different sections within it, and trade unionism is often viewed by its proponents as a means of countering the potential welfare losses which fall on the labour force as a consequence of market imperfections. Let us begin by considering the classic case of monopsony in the labour market.

Monopsony

Monopsony exists in a labour market when there is only one employer of the labour attached to that labour market. The National Coal Board in Britain, for example, is virtually the only employer of coal-miners. We shall use monopsony to illustrate the general case of a labour market dominated by one or more employers who act in such a way as to maximise profits by paying labour less than its marginal product – this is the economic phenomenon of 'exploitation'. (For a full account of the economics of exploitation see Robinson, 1934.) We are subsuming such phenomena as 'oligopsony' and the more mundane partial monopsony under the heading of 'monopsony' – there are few important analytical differences involved.

In neo-classical theory the firm's demand curve for labour, where product markets are imperfectly competitive, is the marginal revenue product schedule of

50

Fig. 5.1

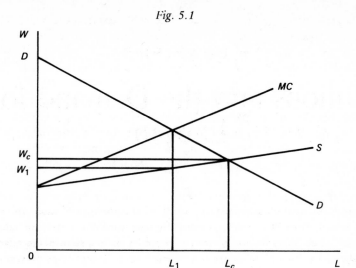

labour, which is the net addition to total revenue expected from the employment of an extra unit of labour. Profit-maximising firms hire labour up to the point at which the marginal cost of labour is equal to the marginal revenue product of labour.

Now a monopsonistic employer — or any firm sufficiently large to influence the wage rate by its hiring of labour — will face an upward-sloping supply schedule of labour. In effect the employer is sufficiently large that in order to attract additional labour at the margin he must offer a higher wage rate than he pays on average to his current employees. We assume labour to be homogeneous here and, for the moment, that the employer pays all of his employees the same wage rate, i.e. he is a non-discriminating monopsonist. Figure 5.1 illustrates the general case of monopsony. The supply schedule of labour to the monopsonist is positively sloped so that the marginal cost of labour is represented by the *MC* curve which is more steeply sloped than the supply (average cost) curve. The employer in this case equates the marginal revenue product of labour and the marginal cost of labour and pays the wage indicated by the supply curve at employment level OL_1, which is OW_1. In a competitive market — where each employer is faced with a perfectly elastic supply of labour, i.e. the average and marginal cost of labour are always equal — employers would equate the supply and demand for labour, which would imply a wage of OW_c and employment of OL_c. Hence the wage rate in the monopsony case is lower than the competitive rate, and employment is also less than in the competitive case.

In a technical sense labour is said to be exploited in this case. Unionism can counter monopsony here without reference to the discipline of the wage/employment trade-off. If the union is able to push the wage rate up from OW_1 to OW_c, it simultaneously achieves increases in wages and employment. Increases in wages beyond OW_c can, however, only be achieved at the cost of reduced employment. When people talk of individual workers having inferior bargaining power relative to employers, and unions in some way 'equalising' bargaining power, it is probably this sort of case they have in mind. (This is sometimes referred to as 'original power'.)

If the monopsonist is able to discriminate between his workers and pay each a wage just equal to his supply price, then he will earn even greater profits and employ more labour. This has a bearing on the topic considered in the last chapter. Unions will in general tend to prevent a monopsonist from discriminating amongst homogeneous groups of labour by applying the principle of 'horizontal equity'.

In practice, employers are rarely able to discriminate in respect of wages to any extent between homogeneous workers. Discrimination normally occurs where the labour force can be segmented by some distinctive characteristic such as sex or colour. The record of the trade union movements in the USA and certain countries in Africa has not always been unambiguous in resisting discrimination on grounds of race or colour but the European trade unions have been fairly firm on this issue. Discrimination on the basis of sex has been permitted and practised by most trade union movements until the last decade. It is now the policy of almost all the European and North American trade union movements to resist sex discrimination, although much remains to be done to make this effective. Of course, unions discriminate when they insist on the same wage rate for workers who differ in efficiency.

In general, therefore, trade unions operating in a monopsonistic labour market ought to have as a minimum objective the establishment of the competitive wage rate. A *single* wage for homogeneous labour is also a necessary objective for unions in order to prevent the monopsonist from discriminating and exploiting.

In practice, because almost all labour markets are characterised by some degree of imperfection which would tend to generate a positively sloped supply curve of labour, the union normally has some scope for countering monopsony-type power without potential employment loss. Hence, the widespread existence of market imperfections which lead to positively sloped supply curves for labour provide an economic rationale, in a welfare sense, for trade union activity so long as unions confine themselves to raising wages and employment to the levels which would prevail in the absence of such imperfections. However, trade unions do not usually see their task as one of establishing 'competitive' wage rates. Unions generally formulate their wage policy in the manner described in chapter 3 with, at least, an implicit recognition of a wage/employment trade-off so that, by definition, they are operating at wage levels which exceed the competitive level.

We should note at this stage that since the union versus monopsonist battle involves distributional issues it raises difficulties for us when we come to consider the question of the welfare costs of trade union activity. We shall return to this in chapter 10.

The elasticity of demand for labour

In the previous two chapters we outlined a framework of trade union wage policy which indicates the supply of labour preferences that trade unions will pursue. At the same time we recognised that the union's preferences will normally be constrained by the demand for labour. In this sense the demand for labour may be viewed as something similar to the budget line in consumer theory. However, it is important to understand that the *elasticity* of demand for labour varies according to industry and occupation in such a way as to allow unions to make large or small wage gains for the exercise of the same degree of union power and to extract larger wage concessions from employers than could be obtained in their absence, other things being equal. It is the most important circumstantial or accommodating variable in determining the size of the wage gains of different unions.

The firm's demand for labour is given by the marginal revenue product of labour, and labour market equilibrium is achieved by equating the marginal cost of labour and the marginal revenue product of labour. We proceed with a simple illustration of the proposition that the elasticity of demand for (union) labour will determine the magnitude of the wage premium which a union can extract from the employer for any given union utility function and degree of power.

The union's utility function is assumed to consist of an internal trade-off between wages and employment. The cost of securing any given wage level is therefore the loss of employment implied by placing the union at the appropriate point on the employer's demand curve. In general, the more inelastic the demand for labour, the lower will be the (employment) cost of securing any given wage rate. This proposition is best illustrated in an indirect way. In fig. 5.2 we consider the wage employment combination which results from equating the same union indifference curve with two demand curves of unequal elasticity. VV' is a union indifference curve and thus everywhere reflects a constant level of utility to the union. Two demand schedules are tangential to VV' to illustrate two equilibrium solutions. Demand curve D_1D_1' is less elastic than demand curve D_2D_2'. The former demand curve is tangential to VV' at X with a wage-employment combination of W_1L_1, and the latter is tangential to VV' at Z with a wage/employment combination of W_2L_2. W_1 is higher than W_2 whilst L_2 is higher than L_1. Hence the lower the elasticity of demand, with the same indifference curve, the greater will be the union wage and the lower the level of union employment.

If we assume all unions to have the same utility function, this result suggests that the relative wage effect of different unions will vary as the elasticity of

Fig. 5.2

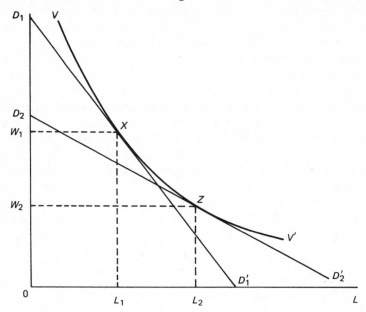

demand for labour varies. There are two analytical aspects to this conclusion. Firstly, unions in industry which face relatively inelastic demand curves for the services of their members will, other things being equal, obtain relatively large wage gains. Secondly, it is a logical inference from this conclusion that an objective of union wage policy will be to make the demand for union labour as inelastic as possible. We assume for the moment that the union will always try to place itself somewhere on the employer's demand curve for union labour.

The determinants of the elasticity of demand for union labour

It is usual in this type of analysis to recall Alfred Marshall's four laws of derived demand and Friedman's subsequent application of them. (Marshall, 1920, pp. 384–6; Friedman, 1951). The four conditions for the derived demand for a factor to be inelastic are:

(1) that the factor be essential to the production of the commodity;
(2) that the demand for the product be inelastic;
(3) that the total costs of the factor relative to total production costs should be small; and
(4) that the supply of the other factors of production should be elastic.

   Let us first note that (3) is not strictly correct and has been criticised and reformulated by Hicks (1932) and Robinson (1934). This condition is popularly referred to as 'the importance of being unimportant'. It only holds, however, where the consumer can substitute more easily than the employer can. More formally, it only holds where the elasticity of substitution is less than the elasticity of product demand, assuming constant returns to scale.

Friedman (1951) discusses these laws in relation to the ability of unions to affect relative wages. Friedman concentrates on laws (1) and (3). He argues that any union effect on wages will normally be small, bigger in the short than in the long run, and important only in the case of craft unions. His case is simply that any factor will be more 'essential' in the short than in the long run, that only craft labour is essential union labour and that only craft union labour accounts for a 'small' proportion of total costs. Ulman (1955) has taken issue with Friedman on a number of points and Reder (1959) has suggested an alternative approach to both of their analyses.

The condition of essentiality

It is clear that the more essential a factor is to the production of a commodity, the more inelastic will be the demand for it. Labour is essential to the production of all commodities, but it is not obvious that *union* labour will be essential to the production of any commodity. This raises the issue of the potential for substituting non-union for union labour which we shall soon discuss at some length in relation to the ability of the union to protect the wage premium of its members. In the short run the demand for union labour will be more inelastic according to the degree to which the union is able to restrict substitution of non-union for union labour. This means that in the short run there will be differences in the elasticity of demand for union labour in different firms and industries according to the degree to which the potential for labour substitution has been restricted. In the long run the potential for substituting capital for labour will make the elasticity of demand for any group of union labour greater than in the short run. However, unions can and do try to restrict the potential for substituting capital for labour — by means of such devices as manning rules, and often a simple refusal to accept new technologies. One need only think of the problems of bringing in new techniques to the printing of newspapers for a dramatic example of this practice.

The product demand condition

It is clear that the more inelastic the demand for a product, the more inelastic will be the derived demand for labour. Unions can normally do little to influence the elasticity of demand for products but they are frequently at the forefront of campaigns to restrict imports of foreign goods competing with domestic ones and thereby to make domestic demand for the domestic product more inelastic. US unions have been particularly active in such campaigns but in Britain and some other European countries unions are developing an increasingly protectionist approach to imports from Japan and third-world countries.

The 'unimportance' condition

'It is important to be unimportant' is a familiar condition for a factor to be facing an inelastic demand schedule. Subject to the Hicks/Robinson definition this is an important condition. It led Friedman to argue that the members of craft unions, who normally represent a small proportion of the workforce in any firm or industry, will face an inelastic demand whilst the members of industrial unions, who are by definition most likely to form a large proportion of the labour force in any firm or industry, face an elastic demand curve. This is a tricky subject and Ulman (1955) has denied Friedman's general conclusion. He first argues that Friedman has neglected the Hicks/Robinson condition although it is not clear that there exist any cases in which that condition would, in practice, alter Friedman's conclusion. Ulman simply asserts that the Hicks/Robinson condition '. . . might obtain in some of the so-called basic industries in which large industrial unions are organised'.

A stronger rebuttal than this is necessary if we are to reject Friedman's view. The second point made by Ulman is that there is a series of relationships of an institutional and conventional kind between the wage policies of different unions within the same industry. This calls into question the meaning of the ratio of the labour cost of any single union group and total labour costs. Ulman argues that it is '. . . the proportion to total variable cost of the wage income of all groups whose wage rates tend, for institutional reasons, to be interrelated'. This is a more substantial criticism of Friedman's view. The most obvious relevance of Ulman's point is illustrated by situations in which a number of different unions, varying greatly in size, within one industry, form a coalition for the purposes of bargaining. Moreover, as we noted in chapter 4, there exist significant interrelations between the wages of different groups of unionised workers which tend to more or less generalise wage gains won by any individual union. The validity of Ulman's argument ultimately depends on the extent to which such considerations prevail in practice. If in fact there is *no* craft or closed union which is able to separately and independently exploit its 'unimportance' in wage bargaining then Ulman is correct and Friedman's argument becomes wholly academic. If, however, there exist craft or closed unions which are capable of exploiting their 'unimportance' in an independent way then Friedman's contention may be correct. This then is not a matter which can be resolved by theory — it is a matter to be determined by empirical methods and, as we shall see in chapter 8, the existing evidence is ambiguous.

The elasticity of supply of other factors

The notion that the elasticity of demand for union labour will be low as the elasticity of supply of the other factors of production (including non-union labour) is high is straightforward. In the event of a fall in product demand, the supply prices of all the factors other than union labour must fall substantially if union labour is to continue being paid the union rate (or anything close to it), since the funds for this must become available from a reduction in the costs of the co-operant factors. The short-run implications of this law depend on the degree to which non-union labour can be substituted for union labour and the degree to which the non-union wage will fall when demand falls. We have suggested that there are distinct limits to the ability of employers to substitute non-union for union labour in practice, and to this extent the law has a restricted relevance. We cannot know, *a priori*, whether labour substitution in any case depresses the union wage by a lot or a little – it ultimately will depend on the extent of substitution, and this in turn has implications for the ability of the union to protect the union wage. So far as other types of labour are concerned – labour which is not a substitute for the union labour under consideration – the issue depends on the extent and strength of union organisation amongst that labour, since co-operant but non-substitutable labour may be well placed to protect its own wage. Circumstances will determine this case. In the long run, capital/labour substitution is possible and the degree of perfection of the capital market will determine whether the supply price of capital will fall sharply enough, as demand falls, to provide the funds required to finance the union wage premium.

The relevance of Marshall's laws

Marshall's laws of the elasticity of derived demand are useful predictive devices. Since our simple model of trade union policy is based on the notion that the cost of obtaining a given wage increase is the employment forgone, then the elasticity of demand is a determinant of the magnitude of the wage increases unions will seek. In general, the more inelastic the demand for union labour, the lower will be the employment cost of winning a given increase in union wages and therefore – if all unions have similar relative tastes for wages and employment and similar objective economic power – the higher will be the actual union wage premium.

The predictive capacity of Marshall's general proposition is fairly obvious. At the simplest level we would predict that unions would gain higher wage premiums in monopolistic industries than in competitive industries, that craft unions would gain a greater wage premium than industrial unions and that skilled labour would tend to gain a higher wage premium than unskilled labour. These predictions are based on a casual impression of the elasticity of demand for different types of labour, and we shall see in later chapters whether or not they are confirmed by empirical evidence.

Labour demand and employers' preferences

Independent of the degree of imperfection in the labour market and the elasticity of demand for labour, we must consider whether employers have preferences about the wage/employment combination that is negotiated and how any such preferences compare with those of unions.

Fig. 5.3

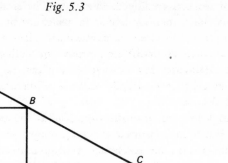

Our proposition is simple and derives directly from the neo-classical theory of the firm. An employer will enjoy increased profits the lower the wage rate, other things being equal. The demand curve for labour is not some sort of employer's indifference curve – the employer enjoys higher utility (higher profits) the further down the demand curve the wage/employment combination is fixed. This proposition holds so long as we make the usual assumption that labour is the only variable factor of production in the short run. We may illustrate this in a simple diagram.

Figure 5.3 simply shows a demand curve for labour and two possible wage/employment combinations which lie on the demand curve. The wage bill is given by the product of the numbers employed and the wage rate; e.g. when the wage is OW_1 the wage bill is $OW_1 \times OL_1$ which is the area of the rectangle OW_1BL_1. The income accruing to the other factors of production is given by the area of the triangle which lies above the wage bill and below the demand curve; e.g. when the wage is OW_1, the returns to non-labour factors are the triangle AW_1B. It is quite evident that as we move down the demand curve from B to C the ratio of the wage bill to total revenue falls and that the absolute amount of revenue accruing to the other factors of production increases. On the assumption of fixed inputs of capital and fixed capital costs, this necessarily involves increasing profits in the short run, the further down the demand curve the wage/employment combination is fixed. (We are also assuming that the employer retains the right to fix the employment level for any given wage rate.)

This proposition seems simple enough and fig. 5.3, while crude, should be sufficient to demonstrate it. Cartter (1959) employs a concept which he calls 'average net revenue product' to illustrate his proposition. This simply involves deducting fixed capital costs from total revenue product and dividing by the number of workers employed. In this way he is able to construct a form of indifference map for employers, in which each indifference curve is at a maximum at its point of intersection with the demand curve and the lower down the demand curve the indifference curve is, the higher the profit level. This is just a more elaborate method than ours of illustrating the general proposition, and the interested (or baffled) reader is referred to chapter 8 of Cartter for further details.

Now employers are normally conceived of as being restricted by the labour supply schedule to a particular wage/employment combination in the competitive model. In that case employers' preferences have no relevance in the analysis since the employer cannot slide down the demand curve to below the point of intersection between the supply and demand curves and will never choose a wage/employment combination above that point if he is a profit maximiser. However, in the context of collective bargaining where unions are seeking to raise wages above their competitive level, employers' preferences are important and in that context the demand curve, or some segment of it, may be regarded as a contract curve. We shall return to this in detail in chapter 7.

This sort of analysis is not so simple when we consider special cases like monopsony in the labour market, but the essential proposition advanced holds in all cases in which rational behaviour is assumed.

Summary

In this chapter we have considered three disparate aspects of the demand for labour which are relevant to the economic analysis of trade union activity. The first issue concerned the market imperfections which result in labour being paid a wage lower than the marginal revenue product by a profit-maximising employer. This situation always arises whenever the supply curve of labour to the employer is positively sloped, since the marginal cost of labour will always exceed the average cost of labour. It also raises the possibility that the employer will discriminate in some measure by paying each worker a wage equal to his marginal cost or, more commonly, by paying groups of workers who are homogeneous in production but distinct in some other characteristic a wage equal to the group's marginal cost. It is these cases which normally lie behind claims that workers have inferior bargaining power compared with employers.

Unions can ensure that workers are paid their marginal product and that discrimination is not practised, simply by pressing for the competitive wage to be paid to all workers who are homogeneous in production. The constraint imposed by the wage/employment trade-off which applies when unions attempt to raise wages above their competitive level is relaxed in this case, since both wages and employment can be raised as the union drives the wage up to its competitive level.

The second issue dealt with was the relevance of the elasticity of demand for labour. We noted that the more inelastic the demand curve facing any given union, the greater will be the wage gain resulting from the application of any given degree of union pressure, other things being equal. Marshall has set out four conditions for the demand for labour to be inelastic, and these have both an analytical and predictive value for our purposes.

Finally we made explicit the fact that employer profitability increases, the lower the wage/employment combination is fixed down the demand curve for labour. This gives us a basis for analysing the determination of the wage/employment combination in collective bargaining when union activity makes wage fixing indeterminate. The demand curve for labour will be shown to resemble a contract curve in collective bargaining.

Further reading

M. Friedman 'Some comments on the significance of labor unions for economic policy' in D. McC. Wright (ed.) *The Impact of the Union* New York, Harcourt Brace (1951).

L. Ulman 'Marshall and Friedman on union strength' *Review of Economics and Statistics* (1955).

M. W. Reder 'Job scarcity and the nature of union power' *Industrial and Labor Relations Review* (1959).

CHAPTER 6

The Extent of Unionisation, Strikes and Union Bargaining Power

In the preceding chapters we have attempted to identify what unions wish to achieve within the economic constraints imposed on them by the market. In this chapter we discuss the instruments which endow unions with the economic power to pursue their objectives. Ultimately this issue hinges on the power of a *collective* organisation of workers relative to the power of *individuals* acting separately. It is the distinction between the market power of an institutional agent and competition in the supply of labour. The economic power of employers is not dealt with in this chapter but is taken up in the next one.

The collective bargaining advantage

If a union is to exert more power in the labour market than individuals acting separately, there must be aspects of collective action which yield advantages over individual action. We shall call this advantage the 'collective bargaining advantage'. Some of its aspects are superficially obvious. For example, we might contrast the power of a union to take action with the power of an individual to quit. This may seem an unambiguous aspect of the collective bargaining advantage but, as we shall see, the matter is not so simple. Hence we shall spend some time in teasing out the various aspects of union activity which may generate a positive collective bargaining advantage.

It is useful at this stage to make some important distinctions. First, it is probably true that the higher the proportion of any given labour force which is unionised, the greater the power of the union to extract wage concessions from employers. However, the extent of unionism is itself a consequence of union power of another kind, since it requires resources and effort to unionise labour and to sustain unionism. We must therefore be careful to recognise that union power is a tricky concept to define in any practical way. Secondly, union power may be viewed as a strictly objective concept – the capacity to inflict economic damage on an employer in order to achieve an aim. It may also be the case,

61

however, that union power is to be viewed as a subjective concept – the willingness of a union to deploy its economic power against an employer. Clearly a 'strong' union with a cautious leader may act quite differently from a 'weak' union with a militant leader, and union 'power' is therefore a function of at least two variables (see Purdy and Zis, 1974). Thirdly, we must distinguish between the actual power of unions *per se* and factors which facilitate the exercise of that power. The elasticity of demand for labour is the prime example but such phenomena as bargaining structure may also be non-neutral factors in facilitating any given degree of bargaining power to yield particular outcomes (see Thomson, Mulvey and Farbman, 1977).

Union power and the extent of unionism

In a general way it is probably true to say that the most significant source of a union's power is the degree of unionisation which it is able to achieve and sustain in the labour market in which it operates. This follows from the proposition, which is conventionally accepted, that the most important source of a union's power is its ability to impose sanctions on employers through industrial actions such as strikes, go-slows and boycotts, or threats of such actions. The effectiveness of these may reasonably be assumed, in general, to be related to the amount of control the union has over the labour force concerned.

Now it is true that there are exceptions to this proposition. However, they are often illusory. For example, if some craft union operating in a largely non-unionised industry represents some vital group of workers, e.g. maintenance engineers, but these are only a minute fraction of the total labour force of the industry, we cannot say that union control of the *industry's* labour force is extensive. But the craft union may wield enormous power since it may be able to bring the whole industry to a standstill simply by calling out its membership on strike. Now this is not necessarily a contradiction of the proposition that the more extensive a union's control over the labour force is, the greater is its power. The *relevant* labour force in this case is the key group of craft workers, and it is essential that *they* should be extensively organised to ensure that the union is powerful in the industry. This is a familiar case in which the membership of the union is not coextensive with the relevant bargaining unit. In general, the proposition relating union power to extent of unionism is true for *the relevant bargaining unit*. For the craft union every firm and industry where wage bargaining takes place is the relevant bargaining unit. For the industrial union the industry or individual firms within it are the relevant bargaining unit. For the general union the unit may be the firm, industry or occupation, or combinations of these depending on the particular case at issue.

Hence the cases in which the general proposition does not hold are normally those in which production methods are such that when one group of workers strikes, the whole production line must close (and the employer must not be able to substitute non-union labour for the strikers). There are other special cases, mainly involving industrial or general unions, where a sufficiently important group of the labour force is in the union and is able to bring all or most production to a standstill. Bearing these reservations in mind let us now proceed to the general question of the economic issues and implications of the extent of unionisation in a labour market.

The ease of substitution between union and non-union labour

We have so far talked of the supply of union labour as if it were insulated from the supply of non-union labour. In some instances this will be the case – e.g. in those occupations and industries in which union membership is effectively a condition of employment – most commonly where there is a 'closed shop' arrangement. However, despite the fact that union shops and closed shops are widespread in the USA and Britain, though less so in continental Europe, there is still in all of the Western industrial countries a 'non-union' sector in the labour force. Now, unless employers are compelled by some sort of closed shop arrangement to hire only union labour, they simply demand 'labour'. If union and non-union labour are available in the same labour market and union labour requires to be paid a higher wage than non-union labour, then employers will presumably attempt to recruit non-union rather than union labour, other things being equal. Similarly, if an employer already employs union labour and the union wins a wage increase which establishes a positive union/non-union wage differential, then the employer will wish to substitute non-union for union labour if that course is open to him and if non-union labour is a good substitute for union labour. Let us consider the implications of this possibility.

Assume that an industry's labour force comprises some union labour and some non-union labour. Further assume that there are two possible situations facing employers: union and non-union labour are perfect substitutes and there are no barriers to such substitution; or union and non-union labour may be perfect substitutes but direct substitution is not open to individual employers because unions can prevent it. In the former case a profit-maximising employer will fire all his union labour and hire non-union labour instead as soon as the supply price of union labour exceeds that of non-union labour. The union labour so displaced will become unemployed and thus form part of the supply of labour in general to the industry, and so long as the total supply of labour to the industry remains the same, the average wage will fall back to its market level. In the latter case, where substitution is not possible, product substitution against the unionised sector will reduce the demand for union labour, thus causing union labour to be displaced and swell the supply of non-union labour. The increase in the supply of non-union labour will reduce the non-union wage and further erode the competitive position of the unionised sector in the product market. This process almost destroyed the United Mine Workers union in the USA in the 1920s when the unionised coalfields rapidly lost their markets to the non-unionised coalfields owing to the erosion of the former's competitive position as the union made rapid wage gains.

We therefore have two possibilities. In a partially unionised industry where direct substitution of non-union for union labour is technically possible, the union may be unable to make any wage gains without risking extinction. In a partially unionised industry in which direct labour substitution is not possible, product substitution against the unionised sector may cause union-won wage gains to be mirrored by falls in the non-union wage as labour is displaced from the union sector to swell the supply of labour to the non-union sector.

The job-rationing problem

We are already in something of a paradox. When the union wins a wage increase for its members, some of them will be displaced from the union sector as a result. At the same time the unionised firms will be paying a premium wage which will attract non-union labour to seek employment in the union sector. This gives rise to the classic 'job-rationing' problem which all unions must deal with. The job-rationing problem is most simply illustrated with the aid of a diagram. Figure 6.1 gives a supply and demand curve for labour with a competitive wage of OW_c. The union wins a wage premium of $W_u W_c$ so that the union wage is OW_u. Now the consequences of the union establishing the wage at a level in excess of its competitive level are that some union workers are displaced from the union sector, the non-union wage will fall below its previously competitive level and a queue of labour — displaced union, non-union and newcomers to the market — measured by the line XZ in fig. 6.1, will form seeking jobs in the union sector. If the union is to prevent the erosion of its wage premium it must ensure that the queue is effectively prevented from entering union employment. Hence the task of the union in the market as a whole is to ration jobs.

Rationing of jobs may in fact be done by employers rather than by unions. When an employer accepts that collective bargaining is to be the method by

Fig. 6.1

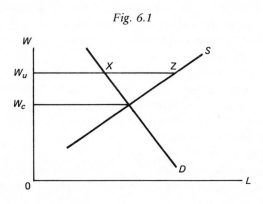

which wages in his firm are to be fixed, then he accepts the wage which is the outcome of that process. When the union wage is accepted by the employer, he then determines the employment level and excludes the queue of surplus labour from employment. Job-rationing by employers will be typical in labour markets which are wholly unionised, and will normally be accompanied by adjustments in production methods to restore long-run profit-maximising conditions. Where this occurs the employer may try to ration on the basis of labour quality so as to offset some of the effects of paying the union wage premium.

When the union is required to perform all or some of the rationing, there are a number of methods open to it. Firstly, craft unions ration jobs by the apprenticeship-system rules relating the number of apprentices to skilled workers and by keeping the wages of apprentices low enough to discourage prospective entrants to the craft. Secondly, in combination with the control of entry afforded by the apprenticeship system, unions can charge high entry fees to prospective new entrants. While this latter practice has virtually disappeared in Britain and continental Europe, instances of it remain in North America. Thirdly, unions can disqualify members of the queue by discrimination – most commonly on grounds of sex. Discrimination is often accompanied by some measure of favouritism, e.g. nepotism, and this may tend to limit the employer's potential to offset high union wages by recruiting high-quality labour.

Non-craft unions are not normally in a position to ration jobs quite so effectively as craft unions are. However, many unions, particularly industrial unions, are able to operate within 'internal labour markets'.* The internal labour market is governed by a system of rules which establish a hierarchy within it. Seniority in the internal job structure is a basic feature of such markets, and job vacancies above the basic entry grades are filled by internal promotion on the basis of seniority. The only way into such a market is at the basic entry grade and this has the effect of limiting the numbers prepared to join the queue. The internal wage structure can also be manipulated to make the entry grades unattractive when the queue is long. While this method of rationing is reasonably effective when the demand for labour is buoyant, it offers very little protection for union members when demand slumps. Moreover, since job security is least amongst those with the shortest service – since lay-offs are inversely related to seniority – the length of the queue will in any case be shorter than it otherwise would be.

Other methods of union job-rationing exist and normally depend on requiring potential entrants to meet standards which arbitrarily disqualify many of them. Discriminatory practices of many kinds are fairly common. They include a refusal to recognise qualifications obtained outside of the union (resisting

---

*Internal labour markets are often thought of as devices used mainly by employers to protect investments in specific training. However, unions will also have a vested interest in the job-security provided by such a market (see Pencavel, 1971).

'dilution'), an insistence on an established status within an employment (e.g. the registration system in the docks) and a variety of restrictive working practices which prevent occupational mobility. It is important to note that these non-price-rationing methods used by unions are unlikely to have the effect of raising the quality of union labour. Hence it would be wrong to infer that the union sector necessarily comprises high-quality labour and the non-union sector low-quality labour simply because there will be queues of applicants for jobs in unionised firms.

There will, however, be many cases in which the union is unable effectively to ration jobs through the sort of mechanisms described and the employer is unwilling to perform the rationing function for the union. In such cases unions may be able to prevent the substitution of non-union for union labour through direct resistance, 'threat effects' and institutional means.

Direct methods against substitution

It is unusual these days for an employer to make a frontal assault on a union by attempting to fire his union labour and replace them directly with non-union labour. In the early stages of trade union development when unions were struggling for recognition and employers were resisting this, it was not uncommon for employers to attempt wholesale substitution of their union labour by non-union workers, and in many cases they were successful. Nowadays trade union recognition is not such a significant issue in industrial relations, and so it is only very occasionally that cases arise where employers attempt to undermine a union by labour substitution. The traditional methods which unions have used to prevent such substitution have been ones of direct resistance.

The history of trade unionism in Europe and particularly North America is peppered with incidents in which strikes, picketing, boycotts and violence against 'blackleg' labour were employed to protect against substitution of non-union for union labour. Such measures may well impose costs on employers outweighing the costs of simply accepting unionism. In addition political pressures, public opinion and, in some countries, legislation have made it difficult for employers to crush trade unions in this way.

The threat effect

There is some evidence to show that, once a union becomes established in a number of firms in industry, the employer reaction in non-unionised firms is defensive and pre-empts any desire to substitute non-union for union labour. This is called the 'threat effect'. The entry of a union into an industry may appear undesirable to employers not at once directly affected by unionisation *not* because of the likely short-run wage effect of unionisation but because their freedom of action on other matters will be constrained by the presence of a union and because it will establish a network of rules, regulations and procedures within the firm. The employer may therefore be willing to pay the union wage rate in order to reduce the demand for unionism from his workforce. If threat effects spread extensively through an industry, then the employers of union labour will not be subject to any significant product substitution against them as a result of paying the union rate, so there will be little incentive to try to crush the union.

Theoretically it is possible that a union with a very small toehold in an industry could, through threat effects, have a very substantial influence on the wage level of the industry and therefore protect its own organisational base. Unfortunately we know little of the extent or nature of threat effects since they are inherently difficult to estimate. One piece of indicative evidence for Britain is worth considering. We have estimates of the percentage of each industry's labour force who are union members (from Price and Bain, 1976). For 1973 we also have data which indicate the percentage of each industry's labour force who are directly or indirectly paid the union wage (*New Earnings Survey*, Department of Employment, 1973). Any difference between these figures will in all probability include the bulk of threat effects although it must not be assumed that it is only threat effects which it reflects. The difference between unionisation data and union wage coverage data will also include such things as non-discrimination in wages within partly unionised plants and firms, and conventional practices by which non-union employers relate their wages to national agreements. However, let us consider the data in Table 6.1.

The selection of industries here is designed to illustrate that in three industries unionisation is very low whereas wage coverage is quite high, whilst the fourth industry is included as a more 'normal' industry in which the difference is small. There are a number of reasons why the first three industries display low unionisation but high agreement coverage; these reasons are obvious and have nothing to do with threat effects. They also illustrate how unions with very low degrees of organisation may be shielded against labour substitution because the union wage is extensively applied to non-union workers. Threat effects must account for some part of this, although we have no way of knowing

Table 6.1   Percentages estimated to be union members and reported to be covered by collective agreements in Britain in 1973, for selected industries

Industry	Union density (1)	Agreement coverage (2)	Difference (2 − 1)
Construction	27.2	78.4	51.2
Agriculture	22.2	40.0	17.8
Distribution	11.4	41.2	29.8
Chemicals	51.2	55.0	4.8

Source: For unionisation, Price and Bain (1976), Table 3; for agreement coverage, *New Earnings Survey* (1973), Tables 110 and 111.

how much — it is, however, reasonable to suppose that it is a substantial element in this situation, since it requires pretty strong assumptions about other effects to account for a significant part of the difference between unionisation and agreement coverage.

We have no way of making similar comparisons for other countries, although I suspect that such large differences between unionisation and agreement coverage as are reported for Britain in Table 6.1 would not be found in many of them. A tentative estimate of a 10% difference between unionisation and agreement coverage for the USA is reported by Ashenfelter (1976).

Rosen (1969) made an ingenious attempt to derive a 'threat-coverage function' for the USA which would indicate the extensiveness of union wage coverage at different levels of unionisation. His analytical method is extremely complicated and is therefore not discussed here. His findings are rather inconclusive — ultimately all that he can say with any confidence is that at high levels of unionisation, threat effects are small. This is what we might intuitively expect since firms which resist being threatened into paying the union rate as unionism progressively becomes more extensive are presumably not going to give in when they have demonstrably survived the growing union challenge. In any case such firms may eventually be ignored by unions because the costs of attempting to organise them may not justify the returns.

The main point here is that while we have very little evidence on the extent of threat effects, there is some evidence and a plausible theory to support the notion that they exist, may be very significant and may protect unions with a small organisational base in an industry from being wiped out by labour or product substitution. In addition, of course, the relative wage effect of unionism is much more extensive, since those workers in threatened firms are paid the union rate as well as union members (see also Flanagan, 1976).

While the threat effect is probably the most important mechanism by which unions in partially organised industries are protected against the substitution of non-union for union labour, there are several other factors also involved. We need not go into detail in describing them since they do not raise issues of economic analysis.

Institutional factors limiting labour substitution

Trade unions in most countries see themselves as part of a trade union movement, and solidarity between unions is often strong. A threat to one union is often seen as a threat to all and this means that the strong, well organised unions can protect the weak ones. This is done in various ways in different countries — partly because of legal constraints — and has also varied a good deal according to historical circumstances. Individual unions themselves, particularly craft unions, have been able to generate internal constraints on the ability of employers to practise labour substitution against their members.

The trade union movement as a whole, or part of it, regularly supports its weaker members by means of sympathetic strikes, boycotts, political pressure and ultimately by a general strike. Examples abound of all of these tactics being employed to ensure the survival of unions under threat from employer attempts to replace union with non-union labour.

Legal factors

The legal framework applying to trade unions in Western countries varies considerably but in many of them trade union rights, particularly in relation to recognition and recruitment, receive some general support from the law. Britain is an extreme case since the rights of unions to establish closed shops and to exclusive jurisdiction are now actually enforceable in law in many cases. In the USA the situation is rather complex. The Taft—Hartley Act, whilst not making union shops illegal, does prevent an employer from firing a worker who is expelled from the union for any reason other than non-payment of union dues. At the same time the Taft—Hartley Act incorporates the unusual provision that State laws on the union shop should take precedence over Federal law. In practice this has resulted in about 20 States having laws which prohibit the union shop. They include, however, only one major industrial State (Indiana) and together account for only 15% of industrial employment. In any case the law is often ignored both by employers and unions. Labour law in continental Europe is varied and complex about trade union rights. In general, it provides for the promotion of free collective bargaining but rarely gives the union rights to enforce union or closed shops. However, in some countries, e.g. Germany and France, the state can direct that the terms of a collective agreement should apply to all workers in the relevant industry irrespective of whether they are union members. This is clearly an important measure for protecting the union against labour substitution. For the rest the law tends to enshrine the rights of unions to organise, to oblige employers to recognise unions and to protect the rights of individuals with grievances against either the union or employer.

Political factors

In most Western countries the trade union movement is allied to the socialist political movement. In France and Italy, however, the majority of unions are affiliated to the communist party, whilst in the USA, only a loose connection between the unions and the Democratic party exists. Political alliances of this kind can be of great benefit to trade unions in limiting employers' activities designed to weaken or undermine their position by substituting non-union for union labour. It is not always so, however. In the USA the Johnson administration was elected with the support of the unions, and one plank in its platform had been the repeal of the controversial Article 14b of the Taft—Hartley Act providing for the rights of states to legislate against union shops. The administration was unable to deliver this particular promise. However, in contrast, in Britain the Labour party has done a great deal to protect the unions. Similarly in other countries — except France and Italy — the union/socialist alliance has tended to be highly favourable to the unions.

A brief conclusion on the extent of unionism and union labour supply

The ability of unions to maintain a supply schedule of labour relative to the market or non-union supply schedule depends on their ability to constrain product and labour substitution against unionised firms in various ways. There is a range of effective instruments, both economic and political, open to the union to establish such protection. The main factors are job-rationing, the threat responses of non-union firms and institutional and legal factors. In the long run, capital/labour ratios will change to accommodate changes in relative factor prices as unions raise the price of union labour to employers. At any given union wage which exceeds the market rate, employment will be less than would obtain at the market wage in both the short and long run.

The sources of bargaining power

We have suggested that, in general, a union will be more powerful in an objective sense, the greater its degree of control over the relevant labour force. Power is the means by which the union extracts from an employer a higher wage rate for its members than could be obtained by them in the absence of the union. We cannot, however, measure *relative* union power in the objective sense in terms of the relative sizes of the wage gains of different unions, since unions will have different utility functions and operate in more or less accommodating economic environments. Let us therefore discuss the instruments of union power in a general way and reserve discussion of relative bargaining power to chapter 7.

Strikes

The centrepiece of the union's armoury is the strike. Unionism itself was established largely by means of the strike and its growth, particularly in the early years, was achieved by the same method. The emergence of unionism amongst unskilled workers is often attributed to the famous 'dockers' tanner' strike in London in 1889, in which non-unionised dock workers found sufficient common purpose to strike, win and create a union. The early growth of unionism involved many strikes in pursuit of recognition of the unions' right to represent their members. It is little wonder that the instrument of power which largely created the modern trade union movement in most countries remains its central weapon.

A strike is a deliberate withdrawal of labour from an employer in order to inflict economic damage on him. This damage will be a short-run loss of profits and in the long run may be a permanent loss of business due to customers switching to more reliable suppliers. Hence the immediate economic force of a strike is to impose costs on the employer in order to coerce him into judging whether the cost of conceding the union claim is likely to be less than the cost of facing the strike. (There are many ingredients involved in that judgment and we shall return to them shortly.)

Strikes also involve the union and its members in costs. The main one is normally the permanent loss of wages for the duration of the strike. Long-run costs may involve lower employment levels if customers permanently desert the employer, and a variety of other costs related to industrial relations matters. As in the case of the employer, therefore, the union and its members must make a judgment about whether the costs of striking are likely to exceed the gains from winning the strike and, again, that is a complex judgment.

We should point out at this stage that the loss of wages involved in striking may be compensated for by income tax rebates, by social security provisions and consequential increased overtime. These vary from country to country and, since they do not affect the general analysis, are not discussed here.

A more important consideration, however, is a type of industrial action which has most of the characteristics of a strike but costs both parties less in any given period of time, though it tends to swing the balance of cost in favour of the union. We mean the so-called 'cut-price' industrial actions, which have gained enormously in popularity as against all-out strikes in Britain in recent years, such as overtime bans, work-to-rules, go-slows and non-cooperation actions. These are analytically similar to all-out strikes (unless they involve the union and its members in no costs). They differ from all-out strikes in that they appear to be relatively more favourable to unions in terms of cost. This may account for Hyman's (1973) finding that most British managers regard cut-price actions as more effective than all-out strikes. Apart from that, they have some obvious advantages to workers over all-out strikes in that a steady income is normally ensured (even if it is less than normal), and workers are therefore able to maintain mortgage and credit commitments which would be interrupted otherwise. Hence, bearing in mind the occasional instances when a cut-price industrial action involves the union and its members in zero costs, the analysis of the cut-price action is subsumed under the general heading of strikes.

Strike threats

A strike, or any other form of industrial action, need not be implemented in order to endow the union with power to coerce an employer. The threat of a strike, so long as it is credible, is almost always present during collective bargaining even though it may never be made explicit. Thus, in the resolution of the vast majority of industrial disputes which never proceed to a strike, the strike threat will normally have been an important determinant of the outcome.

Strike threats, like strikes, affect the position of both sides to a dispute since they imply potential costs to both parties.

Hence the analysis of strikes subsumes the analysis of strike threats, with the important exception of a strike which has as part of its objective the maintenance of the credibility of the strike threat. If a union is forever threatening to strike but never actually does so, employers may begin to suspect that the union is bluffing and act accordingly. So, in order to maintain the strike threat, the union must periodically actually strike unless it is always able to obtain all the concessions it wishes from the employer. Such experiences can, however, be painful and ineffective unless they are fairly regularly practised. The Union of Post Office Workers in Britain became involved in a dispute with the Post Office in 1971 and it was clear that the Post Office did not regard the strike threat as particularly credible. The union struck, ended up accepting a humiliating defeat and has ever since confined itself to more limited forms of activity. In contrast, the United Automobile Workers in the USA normally strike in one major company every time contracts are being renegotiated, so that there is no doubt in anyone's mind about the credibility of their strike threat. Perhaps the National Union of Mineworkers in Britain have recently come closest to the 'optimum' in this matter. Two national mining strikes have taken place since 1972 and they were devastating in their effects. The national strike threat of the mineworkers must now be one of the most intimidating features of British economic and political life. At the same time, this powerful strike threat has been bought in what appears to be a highly cost-effective way due largely to the skill and experience of the miners' leaders.

Strikes versus quits

Unions bargain to set the wage for their own members and not for non-members, and their ability to attract and hold members implies that they should provide a positive wage return to membership relative to non-membership. Their supposed ability to do this is premised on the idea that collective action is likely to be more effective than individual action. This is the so-called collective bargaining advantage. We now explore this matter by following the analysis of Holt (1971).

The strike is an instrument of coercion which depends for its effect on its ability to impose costs on employers. Individuals are rarely able deliberately to impose permanent costs on an employer by a temporary sanction. Few individuals have qualities so scarce that they cannot be replaced, although no doubt there are some. Individual acts of economic sabotage, persistent absenteeism and poor work can be attempted as instruments of individual sanction on employers but are more likely to lead to the courts or to being fired than to successful coercion of an employer. Yet the cost to an employer of a quit, or the potential cost implied by a quit threat, is normally not zero and is often significant. The quit and the quit threat are, therefore, the individual's counterpart of the strike or strike threat. Quits also involve the individual in costs, and quit threats, if they are to be credible, also involve him in potential costs.

Quits

We have seen that the individual is rarely able to inflict any significant damage on an employer by imposing a temporary sanction on him. Unions can inflict significant damage on an employer by imposing the temporary sanction of a strike on him, so that the *collective* strike will always be more effective than the *individual* strike. However, simply because the quit must be a *permanent* action it is more damaging than an individual strike. The cost to an employer of a quit will vary according to the characteristics of the individual involved and also the state of the labour market at the time. The cost of the quit is essentially the cost of replacing the quitter. It is made up of the cost of searching for a replacement — advertising, interviewing, training in some cases — and the costs involved in lost production while a replacement is being sought. In addition, if the quitter is trained and the employer has invested in this, the employer will lose the future stream of returns on his investment in training unless he can find a replacement who is already trained. Other costs involve the loss of the experience of the quitter and, if the employer hoards labour in order to have instant replacements for quitters available, the cost of labour hoarding.

Now in the case of highly skilled and experienced labour — and particularly where the employer has made a major investment in the quitter's training — these costs may be very substantial. However, in the case of a worker who has little skill and/or experience and in whom the employer has invested nothing by way of training, the quit cost to the employer will be relatively small. This will be particularly so when the labour market is slack and there are plenty of potential recruits in the pool of unemployment, but the cost will be relatively high when the labour market is tight and replacement labour hard to come by.

Quits involve costs to workers as well as to employers and these, too, vary according to the characteristics of the quitter and the state of the labour market. The main cost of quitting to the quitter is the loss of income while he searches for a new job. This search also involves costs — some of the more important ones may be psychological rather than financial — and there is always the risk that the quitter may end up having to take a job which pays less than the one he quit. The slacker the labour market, the longer the individual will normally have to search, and the longer the search, the greater the likelihood that he will have to accept a wage reduction. Other things being equal, a skilled worker is generally better placed to find new work at an equivalent wage than an unskilled worker. This is because the labour market is tighter for skilled than unskilled labour in both boom and slump. However, the quit cost to a skilled worker is not necessarily lower than for an unskilled worker since the opportunity cost of search will be greater for skilled than for unskilled labour. Note that a worker who has received specific training — i.e. training of use only to his original employer — is in the same position as an unskilled worker when he quits. Our observations regarding skilled workers, therefore, refer only to those whose training has been mostly 'general', i.e. of use to many employers. There is a special quit cost which falls on specifically trained labour and that is the loss of a part of the individual's wage which is paid specially to discourage him from quitting and depriving the employer of the return on his investment in the training.

The relative cost of quit

The cost of a quit to the employer and to the employee varies with the state of the labour market and may be summarised as follows:

(a) when the labour market is tight (unemployment low) the cost of a quit will be relatively high to the employer and relatively low to the employee; and
(b) when the labour market is slack (unemployment high) the cost of a quit will be relatively low to the employer and relatively high to the employee.

Bearing in mind that different types of workers will be characterised by different *absolute* quit cost considerations, we may generalise and say that the quit *threat* — which is based on the potential relative quit costs — will be most effective when the labour market is tight and least effective when the labour market is slack. On that basis we may illustrate the relative quit/cost ratio — the cost to the company relative to the cost to the worker — in relation to the state of the labour market as in fig. 6.2 (from Holt, 1971). The ratio is measured on the vertical axis and unemployment on the horizontal axis. The curve in the diagram simply shows that when unemployment is low, the cost of a quit falls

Fig. 6.2

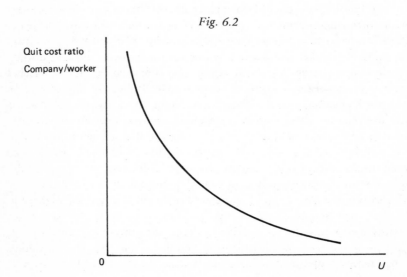

Quit cost ratio
Company/worker

relatively more heavily on the company than on the worker, and that when unemployment is high the cost of a quit falls relatively more heavily on the worker than on the employer.

The cost of a strike to the employer

Let us try to consider the relative costs of a strike in the same way as for quits. To do this we must abstract from the duration of strikes and aspects of strikes which are independent of the state of the labour market (we shall consider these as specific issues shortly). We have already noted some of the general characteristics of strikes, so we shall confine ourselves here to examining how the relative costs of a strike are likely to be allocated according to the state of the labour market.

When the level of aggregate demand is high, company profits are likely to be high also. A strike which occurs when demand is high is therefore likely to impose greater costs in terms of forgone profits on employers than a strike undertaken when demand is low and profits are low. This is a broad generalisation which requires many qualifications but it is probably correct. The qualifications which we must take into account include the level of inventories held by the firm, the possibility that after a strike is over the firm may recoup all the lost profits, and the fact that the firm which is operating during a high-profit period may be better able to withstand a strike.

No doubt some or all of these qualifications will characterise certain firms at certain times. However, unions are aware of these factors and will rarely embark on a hopeless strike if the firm is able to withstand it. Consider, for example, the question of inventories. The coal industry in Britain in recent years has tended to carry fairly high levels of inventories – as have its customers – so that for a strike to inflict real damage on the employer it must last long enough to exhaust the stock of inventories. Hence national coal strikes in Britain typically last a long time and invariably do end up causing economic damage to the employer. So far as the ability of firms to recoup lost profits is concerned, it is hard to find an authentic example. Even where a state-protected monopoly is concerned – e.g. Cement Roadstone in the Irish Republic where imports of cement are forbidden – a prolonged strike will invariably attract substitutes which cause a permanent profit loss to the company. In the case of Cement Roadstone, the Irish government temporarily lifted the ban on cement imports during one protracted strike. The more general argument that in a period of high profits companies will be better placed to withstand a strike does not alter the fact that the strike is normally still more costly in profit terms than no strike at all.

Certain other considerations suggest that a strike undertaken when demand and profits are high will impose relatively severe economic damage on employers. First, a prolonged strike when demand is high – and the labour market therefore tight – may involve the strikers in permanently taking up alternative jobs, and the employer will incur replacement costs when the strike is

over. Secondly, in a period of generally high demand, customers may desert the firm permanently in order to satisfy their own customers. This is the real sharp edge which the policy of the United Automobile Workers poses to the company selected for a strike. All this, taken together with the relatively high profit loss, suggests that the cost of a strike to an employer will be relatively high during periods of high aggregate demand.

Conversely, of course, when aggregate demand is relatively low, then profits will be low, the labour market slack and the likely costs of a strike to the employer relatively low. Hence we may conclude that the costs of a strike to an employer are high when aggregate demand is high, and low when aggregate demand is low.

The cost of a strike to the union

The main cost of a strike to the strikers is the income lost while the strike is in progress. This income loss may be partly offset by any strike pay which the union disburses, and in certain countries this is substantial — in the Netherlands strike pay is 80% of normal earnings — but in others, such as Britain, is normally not very significant. Another source of income to strikers in certain countries is social-security payments made to their families. Neither of these sources of income ought to vary with the state of the labour market, so they should be regarded as a constant offset against the loss of income incurred in strike action. Some strike costs do, however, vary according to the state of the labour market.

When the level of aggregate demand is high, the labour market will tend to be tight. Unemployment will be low and vacancies high. Opportunities for strikers to obtain temporary or part-time work will generally be more readily available in a tight labour market than in a slack one. Hence workers may be able to cushion the effects of the income lost through striking in a tight labour market, but this will be more difficult to do in a slack market. Further, workers who strike when

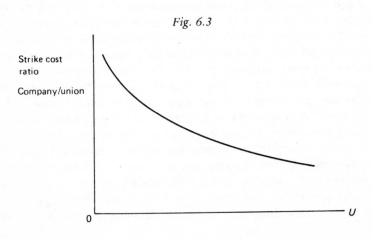

Fig. 6.3

the labour market is tight may take account of the fact that if they wish at any point to withdraw from the strike their prospects of obtaining alternative permanent work are better than they would be in a slack market.

The curve in fig. 6.3 illustrates the points we have discussed. When the labour market is tight (unemployment low) the cost of a strike to the company will tend to be relatively high and the cost to strikers relatively low. Conversely, when the labour market is slack (unemployment high) the cost of the strike to the company will tend to be relatively low and the cost to the strikers relatively high. Hence our curve slopes downwards from left to right in the same way as the quit cost curve in fig. 6.2.

The relative costs of strikes and quits

Theoretically any individual has the option of either quitting or threatening to quit or striking or threatening to strike along with others and ought to choose the more powerful weapon in the circumstances. However, in practice the individual's choice is limited. When the union calls a strike, the quit threat of an individual is inappropriate and is no alternative to strike action — the employer and the union will normally insist on a single bargain being struck. All the same, the collective quit threats of all the union's members may, in extreme cases where the strike threat is insignificant, be invoked. It is more instructive and analytically useful, though, to proceed on the assumption that union members pursue wage claims on the basis of strike threats and that non-union workers pursue their wage claims on the basis of quit threats. Hence we distinguish workers by whether they are union members or not, and their bargaining power is based on the strike threat and the quit threat respectively.

There is no way in which economic *theory* can provide us with a general indication of the relative power of quit threats and strike threats. Holt (1971) asserts that there will be some threshold level of unemployment below which the quit threat becomes more potent than the strike threat. At all levels of unemployment above the threshold the strike threat is more potent than the quit threat. This assertion is illustrated in fig. 6.4, which simply combines figs 6.2 and 6.3 but incorporates Holt's assertion where the threshold unemployment rate is U'. At all levels of unemployment below U' the quit threat carries greater weight than the strike threat and *vice versa* for levels of unemployment greater than U'. What this means in practice is that non-union labour can coerce employers to concede wage increases more effectively than union labour can when unemployment is below U'. Conversely, unions can coerce employers to raise union wages more effectively than non-union individual workers when unemployment is above U'. While this is quite plausible it must be repeated that it is not a prediction of economic theory. However, it is a proposition which has formidable empirical support and on that basis we may accept that fig. 6.4 is probably an accurate description of reality.

The most dramatic piece of empirical evidence in support of Holt's

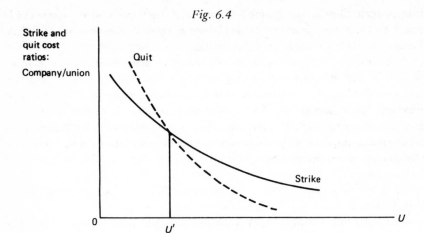

Fig. 6.4

proposition is that the difference between the wages of union workers and the wages of non-union workers, after allowing for any differences due to characteristics unconnected with unionism, is high when unemployment is high, and low when unemployment is low. This wage difference – called the 'union/non-union wage differential' – has been estimated by Lewis (1963a) for the USA for each five-year period between 1920 and 1959 and has been found to vary systematically with the unemployment rate (see Table 8.3 below). Lewis estimated that when unemployment was at its historically highest level, during the great depression of the 1930s, the union wage was about 25% higher than the non-union wage. In contrast, in the years immediately after the Second World War – when unemployment was extremely low – the union/non-union differential was estimated at zero by Lewis. This is, of course, only indicative evidence in support of Holt's hypothesis but there is other evidence which we shall examine in chapter 8 that lends further credibility to Holt.

Now recall fig. 3.7 on p. 36 and look carefully at the relation between the wage preference path (the basis of the union labour supply curve) and the market supply curve (the supply curve of non-union labour). The vertical distance between the two curves indicates the desired union/non-union differential and it may readily be seen that the desired differential will be lowest, the higher the level of demand (the furthest to the north-east in the diagram), and greatest, the lower the level of demand (the furthest to the south-east). While the diagram was deliberately drawn to reflect this relationship, it did emerge naturally from the theoretical considerations employed to construct the wage preference path.

Finally, it is a clear prediction of Holt's proposition that – if they are at all aware of the relative costs of striking under different market conditions – unions will tend to strike most often when the relative costs of striking are favourable to them and unfavourable to the employer, i.e. when unemployment is low. Again there is strong empirical support for this proposition: Rees (1952) has found a strong inverse relation between strike frequency for the USA; Pencavel (1970) has found the same for Britain; and Mulvey (1968) the same for the Irish Republic. Note that we have a paradox here, however. Union strike activity is most intense when unemployment is low, but the union/non-union differential is lowest when unemployment is low and *vice versa*! Does this mean that strikes are ineffective? The answer is, of course, to be found in Holt's proposition regarding the relative potency of strikes and quits. At the same time as unions are employing the strike or strike threat to increase the wages of their members, non-union workers are individually employing the quit and quit threat to increase their wages. Since the quit threat is postulated by Holt to be more potent than the strike threat at very low levels of unemployment, the result is that the union/non-union differential narrows.

Holt's analysis and conclusions are appealing. They are intuitively plausible and are consistent with the empirical evidence. Apart from the general insights which they provide into the complex relation between union activity and market forces, they yield the important conclusion that collective action undertaken by unions will only yield advantages to union members when unemployment is above some threshold level. When unemployment is below that threshold, non-union workers acting individually may in fact secure wage increases larger than those obtained by union workers.

Summary

We have covered a lot of ground in this chapter. The *raison d'être* of trade unions is the idea that collective action is superior to individual action in coercing employers to pay desired rates of wages. We began by considering what it is that is supposed to constitute the 'collective bargaining advantage' and we concluded that collective action must endow individuals with superior economic power than they possess as individuals in dealing with employers if it is indeed to yield an 'advantage'. We proceeded to argue that union power is closely related to the degree to which the union exercises control over the relevant labour force both in order to capitalise on the potential of collective action to win the desired wage and to protect the union-won wage from erosion by market forces. In particular, it appeared that the key to both establishing and protecting extensive unionisation in the labour market — which are the counterparts of winning and protecting union wage gains — is largely to do with the ability of the union to prevent the occurrence of both labour and product substitution against the union sector. 'Threat effects' — where employers pay the union wage rate in order to neutralise any demand for unionisation amongst their workforces — especially tend to limit substitution against the union sector. Moreover, closed- or union-shop agreements, legislation and political factors sometimes serve to entrench unionism.

Once established, the power of a union depends on its ability to inflict permanent economic damage on an employer by means of a temporary withdrawal of its members' services. This is the strike weapon and the threat which strike action implies. Both sides incur costs in a strike, and it is the potential or actual relative costs of a strike which will determine the outcome of bargaining. Unions can minimise the costs of a strike by taking 'cut-price actions' such as work-to-rules, go-slows and overtime bans. Ultimately the union's ability to inflict economic damage on employers lies in its degree of organisation, its resources and its tactics. The analysis of the strike as a determining factor in the outcome of bargaining for the *union* wage — independent of its relation to the non-union wage — is crucially bound up with time considerations and is discussed in detail in chapter 7.

Of more immediate concern to us here is the union's ability to deploy its power so as to win a wage increase in excess of that which individuals using the only weapon available to them — the quit and the quit threat — might secure. Holt has proposed that the quit threat of the individual is a more potent weapon than the strike threat when labour markets are very tight. Conversely, he proposes that the strike threat is the more potent weapon when labour markets are slack. The empirical evidence available to us suggests that he is probably right. This implies that unions may secure wage gains over those which individuals acting alone can secure when labour markets are slack in some measure. Hence the collective bargaining advantage may become negative when labour markets are tight but be positive when labour markets are slack. We take this up empirically in chapter 8 and shall discover that the evidence suggests that unions are in fact able to maintain a positive wage differential over non-union labour in all but the most extreme cases of excess demand for labour.

Further reading

C. C. Holt 'Job search, Phillips' wage relation, and union influence; theory and evidence' in E. S. Phelps (ed.) *Microeconomic Foundations of Employment and Inflation Theory* London, Macmillan (1971).

S. Rosen 'Trade union power, threat effects and the extent of organisation' *Review of Economic Studies* (1969).

M. W. Reder 'Job scarcity and the nature of union power' *Industrial and Labor Relations Review* (1959).

S. Rottenberg 'Wage effects in the theory of the labour movement' *Journal of Political Economy* (1953).

G. S. Becker 'Union restrictions on entry' in *The Public Stake in Union Power* Charlottesville, University of Virginia Press (1959).

N. W. Chamberlain and J. W. Kuhn *Collective Bargaining* New York, McGraw-Hill (1965).

CHAPTER 7

Collective Bargaining

Collective bargaining is the vehicle for the determination of union wages. It is the process by which unions and employers seek to maximise their respective utility and in which strike threats dictate the concessions each side is able to extract from the other. It is also a process bounded by market forces, and it is to this that we first turn our attention.

The economic boundaries of collective bargaining

In chapter 3 we discussed the trade union's utility function and its implications for the supply of union labour, and in chapter 5 we considered aspects of the demand for union labour. We may now bring these concepts together to examine the scope for collective bargaining over wages. In fig. 7.1 we combine the concept of the wage preference path (WPP) — illustrated in fig. 3.6 — and the employer's demand curve for union labour.

We consider the simplest case, where demand has increased since the wage was last fixed. Alternative cases, where demand has remained unchanged or fallen since the wage was fixed, are discussed later. In fig. 7.1 we see a situation in which the wage is fixed at OW and where the WPP intersects the demand curve which existed at the time the wage was fixed, D at Z. Now we assume that the demand for labour has risen to D' and that the employer has increased employment from OL_1 to OL_2 in response to it. If the employer has not increased employment in line with the increase in demand the firm will not be maximising profits. Hence, immediately prior to bargaining, the wage is OW and employment is OL_2. This is the employer's preferred situation since even if the market supply curve of labour is below point Y he is unlikely to try to impose a reduction in the union wage. Now the union's preferences are indicated by the point of intersection between the WPP and the demand curve D' at point Z. At point Z the union's utility is maximised subject to the constraint imposed by the demand curve. Hence we are at point Y on D'; the employer would like to stay there but the union would like to move from point Y towards point Z. The line segment YZ of D' therefore represents a *contract curve*. At any point on the contract curve, both union and employer will be better off than they were at point X on D in terms of utility, although the employer will be worse off than

Fig. 7.1

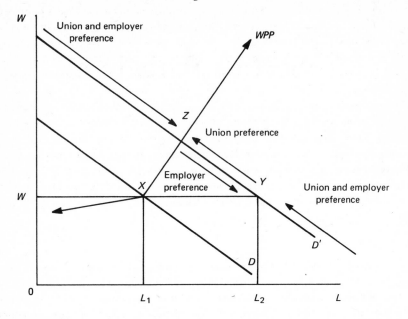

he was at point Y if there is any move along the contract curve towards Z. In
this case it is more sensible to contrast the contract curve with point X since, in
a sense, the employer has enjoyed the benefits of an expansion of demand
without having to pay a higher wage, simply because collective bargaining is a
discrete process – this is more than he could reasonably expect in a non-union
market.

Collective bargaining in this context is simply a process of finding a
wage/employment combination somewhere on the contract curve according to
the relative bargaining power of the two parties. Hence the curve is an area of
indeterminacy in wage fixing and, unlike the conventional model of wage
determination, explicitly permits a set of solutions which maximise the joint
utility of both union and employer. So long as the outcome is a wage above that
indicated by Y, i.e. so long as the union has any bargaining power, the outcome
will be a wage in excess of the competitive wage. (There are some cases in which
this would not be true but they are unlikely to arise in practice.) The cost to the
union of achieving that wage (without striking) is that employment will be
reduced below OL_2 as a result, and the cost to the employer will be reduced
profits. However both sides are likely to be better off than they were at X.
Points Z and Y may therefore be regarded as the economic boundaries which
constrain the scope of collective bargaining. Settlements cannot exceed Z or be
below Y without reducing the utility of one or other party because of the
constraints imposed by the supply and demand curves in the labour market.

This case is a simple one and likely to be the normal situation. The increase in labour demand permits both sides to fix the wage so as to make each better off. It is not, of course, impossible that the demand for labour may remain static or even fall. In these situations there is no scope for *both* parties to be made better off as a result of changing the wage rate. In the case where demand remains static between two bargaining encounters, no change in the wage is likely since any change will reduce the utility of one side or the other. If one side insists on a wage change, the other side may calculate that it is cheaper to accept the reduction in utility rather than become involved in a strike; however, the outcome in such a case is most likely to be a strike. In the case of a fall in the demand for labour the issue involved in bargaining is how to share out the fall in utility between the parties. Unless one party has all the bargaining power and can impose its preference on the other, both parties must accept a reduction in utility. Again, in this situation a strike is quite likely.

Bilateral monopoly

It is not only models of the type illustrated in fig. 7.1, which provide a range of indeterminacy in wage determination bounded by supply and demand constraints. In particular, the neo-classical model of bilateral monopoly gives rise to a range of indeterminacy which provides scope for collective wage bargaining. The bilateral monopoly model is illustrated in fig. 7.2.

This diagram shows a confrontation between a monopsonistic employer and a trade union monopoly. We defer judgment on the realism of assuming that a

Fig. 7.2

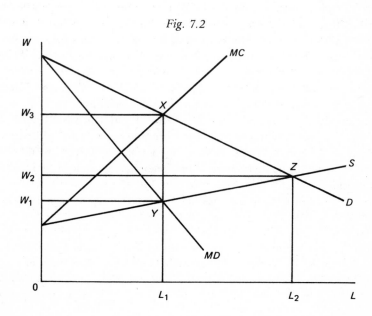

union may be analysed by analogy with a product market monopolist. So far as the monopsonistic character of the employer is concerned, the reader is referred back to chapter 5 for a discussion of this case. The monopsonist is shown in fig. 7.2 to perceive a positively sloped marginal cost curve for labour, and we assume he will wish to maximise profits; this means that he will aim to equate the marginal cost of labour with the demand for labour at point X with a wage rate of OW_1. Now if the union is a monopolistic seller of labour, it will perceive that in order to sell more labour when faced with a negatively sloped demand curve it will have to accept progressively lower rates of pay. Following the analogy with the product market monopolist, the union will restrict sales in order to maximise collective rents by equating the supply curve of labour with a curve which is marginal to the employer's demand curve, i.e. at point Y where $S = MD$ and the wage is OW_3.

In this situation the profit-maximising solution for the employer is OW_1, the rent-maximising wage to the union is OW_3, and the two are rather far apart. Hence a range of indeterminacy appears to exist between OW_1 and OW_3, and this implies scope for collective bargaining. Joint utilities are maximised at the competitive wage OW_2 but for the union this is no different from simply countering monopsony. Hence the wage will be fixed according to relative bargaining power, and all that we can know *a priori* is that it will lie somewhere in the range $W_1 W_3$.

The bilateral monopoly model has a certain theoretical appeal but it is difficult to accept the assumption that a union will behave by analogy with a product market monopoly. The main objection to this view is that a business monopoly sells goods, the production of which involves it in costs. The union is not selling labour in the sense that it requires a return covering the costs of producing that labour. The union is only the agent of sale on behalf of individuals who incur their own costs in or out of work. This suggests that the union will have little appreciation or concern for the marginal supply prices of its members and will therefore not seek to maximise collective wage rents. This has led Reder (1952) to suggest that the bilateral model '. . . is of dubious help . . .' in the analysis of wage determination, and Dunlop (1950) to describe it as '. . . an object of analytical interest but without any readily discernible counterpart in trade union policies'. There are other objections to the bilateral monopoly model, but those already stated are sufficiently forceful to allow us to treat it as one of limited interest and relevance to unions and to wage determination.

Alternative approaches to the question of indeterminacy in wage fixing which allow scope for collective bargaining within otherwise conventional models — such as 'oligopsony', rigid coefficients of production, and interdependence of supply and demand curves — are only of historical or peripheral interest and the reader is referred to Cartter (1959), Dobb (1929) and Robertson (1931 and 1957).

Models of the collective bargaining process

All we have said so far is that theoretical considerations suggest that areas of indeterminacy in wage fixing will occur when certain reasonable assumptions are made about trade union behaviour. The area of indeterminacy is essentially a range of wage possibilities which are not ruled out by market forces as viable economic solutions — although all but one are sub-optimal from a welfare standpoint. Unions and employers bargain within these bounds to determine a wage, and market forces subsequently determine the level of employment which will be associated with the wage outcome so long as the employer is free to fix the level of employment. Employers and unions invariably wish to fix the wage at opposite ends of the contract curve, so that bargaining consists of a process by which each side seeks to extract concessions from the other until some mutually agreeable compromise emerges. The extent to which concessions may be extracted depends largely on the balance of the strike threat or on the attrition of the strike itself should bargaining break down and hostilities commence.

We shall discuss strikes and strike threats in terms of the relative costs to both parties of agreeing or disagreeing on a compromise. This analysis should not be confused with that in the previous chapter where we discussed quit and strike threat costs. There we were concerned to demonstrate an element in the determination of the union wage relative to the non-union wage; here we are concerned only with the general determinants of the union wage for any given strike cost ratio.

The costs of agreeing and of disagreeing

The conventional approach to collective bargaining focuses on the relative costs of agreeing to some compromise wage as against those of disagreeing. Chamberlain (1951) and many others since have expressed the bargaining power of each side in the following simple way:

$$\text{Union's bargaining power} = \frac{\text{Cost to employer of disagreeing with union}}{\text{Cost to employer of agreeing on union's terms}}$$

$$\text{Employer's bargaining power} = \frac{\text{Cost to union of disagreeing with employer}}{\text{Cost to union of agreeing on employer's terms}}$$

We assume that both parties are rational economic agents and therefore wish to emerge from bargaining with the outcome which involves the minimum costs. Further, we assume that both parties have taken *all* foreseeable costs into account, including the relevant probabilities of various potential costs, and have discounted all costs where appropriate. In that case the simple general rule which emerges is that where the cost ratio is greater than one, the party will choose to agree to the other's terms and, where it is less than one, the party will choose to disagree with the other's terms.

Is this a realistic basis for economic analysis?

In the previous chapter we analysed the main costs which unions and employers are likely to incur if they choose to disagree. These were considered in the context of quit cost ratios and strike cost ratios as though they occurred at a point in time. In order to expand on the costs of agreeing and disagreeing we need to look into the future. Before doing so, we must consider the realism of this procedure. The implications of the cost ratios are that unions and employers can make accurate estimates of the costs of this or that particular item and, more particularly, are able to project these costs into the future with the appropriate probabilities applied to them and the correct discount rate used to convert them into current values. Many economists have been critical of this approach on the grounds that fine calculations of this kind simply cannot be made and continuously revised with anything like the accuracy which would be required to make them into effective tools of decision making (see, e.g., Boulding, 1963). Moreover, where cost/return analyses have been undertaken after a strike has occurred, they invariably show that each side would have been better off if it had accepted the final pre-strike offer of the other side (see, e.g., Cyriax and Oakeshott, 1960). This latter approach is usually criticised by trade unionists for failing to take account of the need to maintain a credible strike threat in the calculations, and that is a valid point. However, common sense or any experience of the conduct of strikes tells us that fine cost calculations are *not* in practice either the only or most important determinant of the behaviour of the parties to an industrial dispute. In the first place, all sorts of subjective factors ranging from frustration to sheer vindictiveness play an important role in determining the course of collective bargaining and strikes. Secondly, often the parties have no information on which to make the relevant cost calculations. Now, if we are to proceed along the lines of a rational cost-based analysis of bargaining and strikes, we must make a judgment about its realism in view of what has just been asserted.

Boulding (1963) observed that 'the strike cannot be treated as the economist would like to treat it, as a rational phenomenon, in which each side nicely calculates the expected benefit of another day's strike and weighs this against an equally nicely calculated loss'. Clearly he is right. However, unions which have had experience of bargaining with a particular employer over time and who have been involved in strikes against him develop an instinctive feel for his flexibility, his ability to bluff and for his reaction when the chips are down. The employer or his managers acquire the same kind of understanding of the union. Now a large part of this 'instinctive' understanding of the other party provides a basis for a rough assessment of the costs involved in any particular course of action.

For example, if some union is known to be likely to strike unless it obtains $X\%$ of its first demand across the bargaining table and is also known to be likely to strike for a very long time in order to get at least $Z\%$ of the original claim, the employer is reasonably well placed to put a rough cost on failing to concede the $X\%$ in the first place. The National Union of Mineworkers in Britain and the United Automobile Workers in the USA would approximate fairly closely to this description.

What we are suggesting is that, whilst it is not likely that precise cost calculations characterise the bargaining process and decisions to strike, it is reasonable to suppose that rough estimates based on judgments which are the product of experience probably do provide the basis for the conduct of bargaining and strikes. Sometimes these judgments will prove to have been hopelessly inaccurate — usually where experience is lacking — and one side or the other will embark on a disaster course as a result. However, the vast majority of collective bargains yield outcomes which are peaceably arrived at and represent a reasonable compromise. Similarly, where strike action is undertaken it is unusual to find one side totally defeated. This generalisation indicates a fair degree of rationality in the course of bargaining and striking, which is consistent with a tolerably accurate assessment of the costs and returns associated with the tactics employed by each party. We should note here that the above observation about the cost effectiveness of strikes is not inconsistent with this view. A strike may, in the period in which it is undertaken, be more costly to both parties than not striking and instead accepting the other's demand. However, in subsequent periods strike-free bargaining may yield satisfactory compromises for many years, precisely because the lessons of resorting to strike action were learned. Hence, over the longer period the losses due to any particular strike may well be recouped by the lessons learned from it.

It is on this basis that we now consider bargaining models. We recognise that only rough and ready calculation of the costs and returns to various bargaining strategies can be made. We further recognise that there will be a significant element of irrational (subjective) economic behaviour involved in bargaining. However, we assume that it remains useful to uncover the precise calculations which, if they were possible, would determine bargaining tactics, in order to provide a basis for the economic analysis of the process. This is only a slightly stronger assumption than is made in many other branches of economics where we proceed on the assumption that economic agents behave *as if* they were rational economic men with access to full information.

The costs of agreeing
We have already noted in chapter 6 the main aspects of the costs to each side of *disagreeing*. The costs of *agreeing* are rather harder to pin down — particularly for the union. In general, it is reasonable to assume that from the employer's point of view the costs of agreeing to any particular settlement are the permanent loss of profits implied by the wage concession involved. Industrial

relations issues and questions about the employer's credibility in bargaining also arise but are less tangible. From the union's point of view the costs of agreeing would, by analogy, be the permanent loss of its members' wage income implied by making the concession required for a peaceful settlement. This is a tricky issue since it once again highlights the difficulties of treating an agent as though it were the direct seller of union labour. The institutional character of the union becomes paramount here. The union negotiators must balance any concessions to the employer against the likely response of their members, and in that sense they stand between two principals. Management are rarely in a similar position. While company boards may take an active interest in the outcome of wage negotiations, the real rank and file — shareholders — are normally remote from such issues. Proposed settlements are often rejected by union members but never by shareholders. This is the context in which Ross's (1948) view of the union as a political entity with an institutional identity distinct from that of the membership and with a leadership which has its own objectives and preferences becomes very relevant.

The cost of agreeing may in some instances actually represent benefits to the union members if they feel their leaders to be overambitious — they are saved the costs of a strike from which they expect no real returns. Conversely, they may be deeply aggrieved by an agreement which they perceive to be much lower than was feasible and may also feel that they have lost face, status and credibility as a result. In the former situation the members may reject their leaders' call for a strike, and in the latter may reject the contract or proposed contract. The union leadership must obviously try to please the majority of their members but may, for example, wish to create a militant image of themselves and try to drag the membership along with them in pursuit of that ambition, or they may wish to create a moderate image of themselves and try to contain the aspirations of their members. Hence there are costs of agreeing (positive or negative) which fall on the union leadership and which are more or less independent of the costs to their members. The union itself may find it imperative to agree because its leaders may feel that it is too weak — perhaps financially or organisationally — to countenance a strike. Conversely, the union may find it necessary to agree to a settlement lower than could be obtained, because it would incur the wrath of other unions who are observing some policy on wages agreed with government. Here the costs of agreeing (positive or negative) fall on the union as an institution and are more or less independent of the membership or leadership. There are obviously many permutations of the costs of agreeing and on whom these costs fall. The complexities of resolving these essentially political problems of unions are beyond the scope of this book, but we must be aware that they are subsumed under the innocuous term 'costs of agreeing to the union' and that they could very well dictate tactics not easily explicable in terms of conventional economic analysis.

It is worth noting here that it is sometimes argued that on occasions strikes actually benefit one or both sides. One situation in which the strike benefits the employer is when there is a temporary excess capacity in the firm or industry, and workers would have to be temporarily laid off and paid for a time. In such a case employers may have no fear of a strike or actually provoke one. Hyman (1973) cites the example of Chrysler: a strike occurred in their Coventry plant when '. . . management, faced by a shortage of bodies from the Linwood factory, sent defective panels down the line and then docked the employees' pay for "shoddy work". The need to give lay-off pay was avoided by the strike which they provoked.' It is also argued that strikes may benefit both parties by 'clearing the air' or generally permitting frustrations and unspoken grievances to surface and be dealt with and thus creating a better industrial relations atmosphere afterwards (see, e.g., Walton and McKersie, 1965).

A further point to note is that strikes are often not about pay at all. Many relate to issues of seniority, discipline, dismissal, procedures and physical conditions of work. These are in many respects similar to 'economic' strikes from an analytical point of view, but are best approached from an institutional or sociological standpoint if they are to be properly understood.

A simple bargaining model

Collective bargaining is a process of negotiation in which unions and employers attempt to arrive at some compromise between their respective preferences. Each party proceeds on the basis that a failure to arrive at a peaceful compromise will result in a strike with all its associated costs, so that the strike threat hangs over the heads of the bargainers throughout negotiations. Hence the potential costs of disagreeing relative to those of agreeing, the strike threat, determine whether or not a strike actually results. Unless one party actually wants it, a strike will only occur when the expectations of the two parties about the costs and returns of strike action diverge substantially. This is so, in general, because it is cheaper for both sides to avoid strike action.

The simplest bargaining models are variants of the Hicks (1932) model (see fig. 7.3). The employer is depicted as behaving in accordance with a 'concession curve', EC, which is determined by the cost of agreeing to pay the union the wage they demand as against the cost of refusing. The concession curve, therefore, must be expressed in terms of the expected length of any strike which constitutes the costs of disagreeing. Now as time passes and costs are anticipated to accumulate to the employer, his concession curve will slope upwards from left to right since it represents the locus of all wage settlements he will be prepared to concede in order to avoid a strike of a given length. Hence the expected cost of agreeing is equal to the expected cost of disagreeing at all points on the concession curve.

The employer's concession curve is the curve EC in fig. 7.3. The employer would concede wage OW_e to the union if the union had no credible strike threat. That is approximately the same as conceding wage L_2Y in fig. 7.1. However, if the union is expected by the employer to strike for OT_2 days, then the costs of

Fig. 7.3

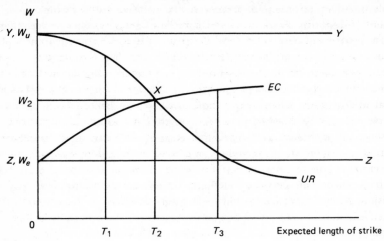

conceding wage OW_2 are equal to the costs of the strike. If the union pitches its wage claim anywhere below the EC curve, then the employer will immediately concede it since the costs of so doing will be less than the costs of a strike of the duration expected at that point on his concession curve. The employer's concession curve eventually becomes horizontal since there will be some wage rate at which the employer would rather go out of business than concede the wage demand.

The curve UR is the 'union resistance' curve and is the locus of all the wage rates which the union would accept rather than strike for the time expected to secure that wage. The union resistance curve begins with wage OW_u – approximately the same as wage Z in fig. 7.1 – which will only be achieved if the employer is not prepared to contemplate any strike action. If however the union expects to have to strike for OT_2 days in order to secure wage OW_2, then the costs of resisting the employer's lower offers are equal to the costs of striking for the required period of time. The union resistance curve may be nearly horizontal over a range which represents the union's perception of some minimum wage to which its members are 'entitled', but ultimately the curve will cut some horizontal line ZZ which represents the point at which the union cannot sustain strike action any further, whatever is being offered.

These are reasonably simple concepts which portray the strike threat or strike as a calculated decision by both parties to extract concessions in such a way as always to equate costs. The employer's concession costs are given by the area between the concession curve EC and the line ZZ, and the union's concession costs are given by the area between the UR curve and the line YY. Equally these cost areas represent the costs of a strike to obtain any given wage. It is implicit in this analysis that each side is aware of its own concession or resistance curve but must make an informed judgment about that of the other side.

There are shortcomings in this type of approach. It is implied that there is only one point at which the concession and resistance curves intersect — X. Now if both sides form a fairly accurate impression of each other's concession curve, then a strike will not take place — both sides will agree to settle for wage OW_2. This assumption would be consistent with the fact that most wage negotiations never proceed to strike action. However — since strikes do happen from time to time — their actual occurrence can only be explained by an assumption requiring that one or other side misjudges the concession curve of the other or that the curves are not stable over time or that irrational factors are involved in the dispute. All of these are possible in practice. We have already accepted that the sort of cost calculations implied in concession and resistance schedules can only be crude approximations in real life. Hence, the scope for misjudging the other party's concession curve is likely to be substantial and, where significant misjudgments are involved, strikes will occur. Moreover, in the course of a strike itself the parties may revise their expectations of the other's behaviour as the strike proceeds and as they acquire more information — then, concession and resistance curves will be displaced and the final settlement will not be the expected one.

It is perhaps most realistic to understand concession and resistance curves as ranges of points within a tunnel rather than as lines; see fig. 7.4. The two curves are now translated into broad ranges of possible expected outcome; this reflects the limitations on either side against knowing in practice the precise location of the other party's or their own concession curve. Note that this allows for a settlement at one of a range of wage rates and for it to be reached over different time periods of strike action.

Hicks argued that 'adequate knowledge will always make a settlement possible', and that strikes only occur when one side or the other has inadequate knowledge or negotiations are poorly conducted. However, so long as we accept that expectations differ between the two sides and that changes in the position of each side may occur in the course of negotiation (or strike), then from the outset no determinate settlement need exist and strikes may occur. Hence the

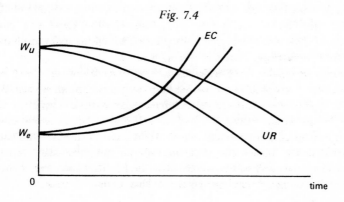

Fig. 7.4

Hicks model is rather too formal and demanding in its assumptions to portray the real world. We may proceed by recognising the limitations of the Hicks model but nevertheless accepting it as a useful tool of analysis so long as it is applied in a flexible and relaxed way. Others have chosen to refine the model further – mainly by introducing mathematical game theory – in order to make it even more formal and determinate (see de Menil, 1971, for a good survey of such models). Such models are, no doubt, elegant exercises in economic and mathematical analysis but are of limited value in advancing our understanding of the collective bargaining process.

Most bargaining models employ the concepts of the costs of agreeing and the costs of disagreeing as the basis on which both parties behave in bargaining. Few such models are both determinate and realistic. Ultimately negotiating skill, toughness and sheer bullying, all enter into the final settlement arrived at and these cannot be measured in such a way as to be incorporated into bargaining models. This calls for a more behavioural approach to collective bargaining than economic models alone can provide. Moreover, all of the economic bargaining models are based on the assumption that there will always be some fixed amount of utility to be conceded and the only point at issue is how that utility is to be shared between the two sides. Earlier in this chapter we noted that there may be no increased utility – or even reduced utility – to share out since the last bargain was struck and in such cases economic bargaining models appear to have no relevance. Again, a behavioural approach to bargaining is a useful alternative way of looking at the process since it can more easily accommodate such situations. Walton and McKersie (1965) have mapped out the essentials of such a model and we now consider some aspects of their approach.

A behavioural model of bargaining

The Walton and McKersie (W and M) bargaining model is largely concerned with the sociological and psychological aspects of the process. While these are clearly of great importance in obtaining a comprehensive understanding of the collective bargaining process they fall outside the scope of this book – we subsume them under such concepts as the 'internal trade-off' in the union's utility function and the political variables which intervene in bargaining. However, there is an interesting economic dimension to their model.

W and M distinguish between those situations in which there is a limited amount of utility available to be shared between the parties and those in which the parties themselves may act in such a way as to determine both the amount and distribution of the utility involved. The former are called 'issues' and are subject to 'distributive' bargaining tactics, while the latter are called 'problems' and are subject to 'integrative' bargaining tactics. This distinction is one that goes beyond the analysis of the conventional bargaining model and allows us an insight into the actual operation of collective bargaining.

Fig. 7.5

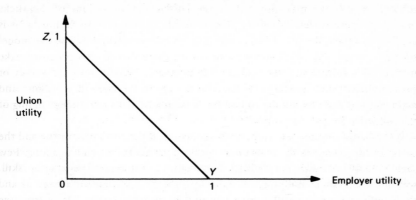

Distributive bargaining is assumed to be the only type of bargaining carried on in conventional bargaining models. It occurs when there is a fixed (positive, negative or zero) amount of utility to be distributed between the parties, and its main characteristic is that each party can only gain what the other party loses. The analysis of distributive bargaining tactics is not significantly different from the analysis involved in the Hicks model discussed already. Hence the pure distributive case may be illustrated as a contract curve, which may be conceived of as lying between points Z and Y in fig. 7.5.

The line ZY is a straightforward contract curve bounded by the economic constraints outlined at the beginning of this chapter. The union can only increase its utility by moving down the line from Z towards Y, which progressively reduces the utility available to the employer. Conversely, the employer can only increase his utility by moving up the line from Y towards Z at the expense of the union. Hence all moves in the distributive case involve conflict. Its resolution hinges on a number of factors. If, as in the cases we have considered so far, there has been a discrete increase in the total utility available to be shared out between the parties since the last bargain was struck (e.g. because demand has increased), then a Hicks-type analysis is appropriate. Gains will be shared in proportion to the relative bargaining power of the two sides and their respective utility functions.

Now when there is no increase in utility since the last settlement to be shared out (in real terms), both sides are likely to attempt to maintain the *status quo* unless their utility functions have altered in the interim. If there is significant money illusion this may, in practice, be achieved by simply adjusting nominal wages in line with the rise in the cost of living and thereby maintain the real wage at its old level. Alternatively, a struggle will ensue which involves one or other side in being made *absolutely worse off* in real terms. Unless there are long-term considerations which favour such a situation this will almost certainly be achieved only by strike action. This is sometimes called a 'zero-sum game'.

In a growing economy this is not likely to be a common case. Economic growth normally provides for increases in the utility of all parties over time, but in certain time periods — such as the mid-1970s — growth may provide no room for real increases in utility and in any case there will always be some industries or firms in which circumstances preclude increases in utility for any party. Hence in the extreme case where there is actually a fall in the utility to be divided between the parties — as was the case in 1975 and 1976 in Britain — the issue to be determined by bargaining is how to share out the fall. In such situations unions are generally concerned to minimise the fall in the real wage — even at the expense of high levels of unemployment — and since unions are typically weak when the labour market is slack, strike-free settlements are likely where unions are able to trade employment for wages, but strikes are likely where employers insist on wage cuts.

In contrast to the situation where the parties are faced with some fixed amount of utility to share out, there will be circumstances in which both parties, by their joint actions, may increase the total utility available for distribution. Such circumstances are said to have 'integrative potential', and bargaining is directed towards a 'problem' rather than an issue. Figure 7.6 illustrates a utility frontier in which integrative potential exists. The utility frontier has a unique point on it, X, at which *both* parties are better off than they could be anywhere else on the frontier and better off than at their preferred (distributive) maxima Z and Y. However, in order to reach X both union and employer must realise the integrative potential of the situation. In practice, integrative potential will normally exist where some innovation in work or production methods is available to increase efficiency, revenue or profit. For example, unions often employ restrictive work practices which, if abandoned, could permit both sides to raise their utility beyond that which is in any case available to them. Productivity bargaining in Britain, which was common in the early 1960s, was a good example of this. The union agreed to introduce flexible work rules and to eliminate much overtime working in return for substantial wage increases. The

Fig. 7.6

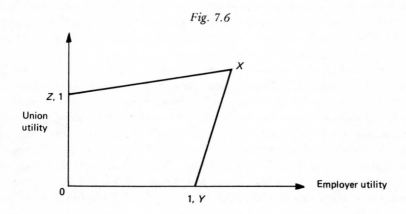

union therefore gained in net utility to the extent that the wage increase outweighed the loss of utility involved in surrendering its control over labour deployment. The employer gained in utility to the extent that a more efficient deployment of labour reduced unit labour costs and outweighed the increase in wages he was required to pay. Hence both sides by their joint action were able to push the utility frontier out to point X. Judging by the popularity of productivity bargaining in Britain – between 1965 and 1969 a quarter of all workers in Britain were affected by productivity agreements – there must have been considerable integrative potential in British industry. Other examples of integrative potential involve the innovation of new technology, joint problem-solving arrangements and so on (for an excellent US perspective on certain of these issues see Healy, 1965).

A third case involving mixed integrative and distributive bargaining also exists. Figure 7.7 illustrates the utility frontier in the mixed case. Here there is an element of distributive and integrative bargaining potential. Joint utility is uniquely maximised at point X but it remains possible for either party to increase their own utility to a level higher than at X by engaging in distributive bargaining tactics. Hence the employer is better off at any point between Y and X but this calls for a disproportionate sacrifice on the part of the union. Similarly the union is better off anywhere between Z and X but again this imposes a substantial sacrifice on the employer. The probability is that in mixed cases of this kind, so long as both sides recognise the nature of the situation, fairly direct progress will be made to settling at point X.

The foregoing is in no sense intended to summarise the W and M model – it is instead designed to pick out a schematic device employed in that model as a useful illustration of the economic framework of collective bargaining. The W and M model, as presented here, is not an alternative to the conventional bargaining models of the Hicks type. Bargaining tactics will for the most part be guided by the same considerations in both types of model – however, the W and M model does go beyond the pure conflict situations implied by the

Fig. 7.7

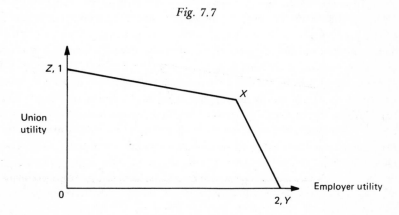

conventional bargaining models by introducing the concept of integrative bargaining potential. The addition of this simple concept adds a new dimension to the bargaining process since it treats bargaining as having the potential to *create* utility as well as to distribute it.

The structure of collective bargaining

Collective bargaining is often thought of as simply a mechanism in which unions and employers negotiate and compromise on wage issues. The *structure* of collective bargaining is seen as neutral or irrelevant in this process. In short, collective bargaining is a process, not a structure of activities.

Now this view of the bargaining process is not in fact tenable. The structure of collective bargaining does appear to be a factor which affects the outcome and is therefore worthy of consideration. First, however, there is the problem of defining what we mean by the structure of collective bargaining.

The process of collective bargaining is carried on in different countries at different levels with more or less extensive coverage. For example, in Sweden collective bargaining is conducted in a highly centralised way whereby the central trade union congress, the LO (equivalent to the TUC in Britain and the AFL/CIO in the USA) negotiates a 'framework' agreement to cover the entire union membership. This framework agreement is later subject to modification at workshop level to meet the needs of particular plants. In contrast, in the USA and Britain collective bargaining is relatively decentralised, with a large number of individual bargaining units in which individual unions and employers negotiate plant, industry and company agreements. Moreover, within the decentralised systems of bargaining, there exist various layers of bargaining such that an individual union worker may have his wages determined by a number of different agreements each built on to another.

The classification of bargaining structure into an operational economic concept is difficult since economic theory has little to say about the structure of bargaining. Moreover, we are severely restricted by the availability of information about the structure of bargaining and its economic consequences in carrying out any empirical tests of plausible hypotheses. However, some work had been done on this topic for both Britain and the USA and we may briefly outline the main concepts involved.

First let us simply define a 'bargaining unit' as any forum of collective bargaining in which settlements of employer/union disputes may occur. Hence a national union/employer negotiating body is a very formal bargaining unit but, equally, an individual shop steward/junior manager also constitutes an effective bargaining unit. The structure of collective bargaining is the configuration of bargaining units which constitute the total system. Now there are various ways in which to group bargaining units into reasonably homogeneous classes which are economically relevant. In Britain, for example, the Donovan Commission

(1968) chose to distinguish between the 'formal' (official national industry-wide bargaining system) and the 'informal' (workshop bargaining system which supplements national agreements). This is a fairly fundamental method of describing the structure of collective bargaining in Britain since it distinguishes between the economic outcomes of national bargaining and national-plus-supplementary bargaining – a distinction which has economic relevance as we shall shortly see.

Clearly other descriptions of collective bargaining structure will also have an economic relevance. Chamberlain (1961) has described bargaining structure in the USA primarily in terms of bargaining coalitions which find their rationale in the desire of unions to minimise the potential for either product or labour substitution against the unionised sector. Industrial unions tend to restrict the potential for product market substitution and craft unions restrict the potential for labour market substitution. Within such coalitions, however, special interest groups – whose interest is not identical with the entire coalition – exist and find expression in formal or informal bargaining units which are subsidiary to, and contained within, the coalition. This is the phenomenon of workshop bargaining by stewards. On this view we require to go a little beyond the distinction made by Donovan and recognise that bargaining *jurisdiction* is an additional aspect of bargaining *level* in the concept of bargaining structure.

Chamberlain's approach immediately leads us towards a description of bargaining structure which relates the jurisdictions of both the employer's bargaining unit and the union's bargaining unit as well as the levels at which these function. On the employer's side we might distinguish jurisdiction according to whether the employer acts in concert with other employers in negotiations, acts alone but in respect of a number of plants, or acts alone in respect of a single plant. At the same time we need to take account of the levels at which negotiations take place – primarily the distinction between industry, company, plant and workshop levels. Clearly jurisdiction and level of bargaining are similar, but it is useful to maintain a conceptual distinction between them because several levels of bargaining (subsidiary jurisdictions) may be contained within a single primary jurisdiction.

On the union side one may also determine various jurisdictions ranging from small craft unions which operate independently within an industry or plant, to the large alliances of unions which come together to negotiate at industry level. Levels of bargaining also vary from industry-wide national bargaining to workshop bargaining. In the main the structure of bargaining is based on employer and union counterparts – employers from industry-wide alliances negotiate with industry-wide union coalitions, and a supervisor or junior manager negotiates with shop stewards. However, this is not always the case and there are many examples of a single employer negotiating with an industry-wide union – e.g. the large automobile companies in the USA – or a coalition of employers negotiating with a single craft union – e.g. newspaper owners and journalists. In fact the permutations of the composition of the two sides in

Table 7.1   Percentage of labour force
covered by various agreement types in
Britain, 1968*

Agreement type	Males	Females
National/industry	64.1	61.6
District	2.3	1.5
Company	26.0	23.8
Plant	4.9	3.2
Workshop	4.0	3.3

Source: New Earnings Survey, 1968,
Tables 131 and 132.

*Since individuals may be covered by more
than one agreement type, the figures do not
sum to the total percentage covered by
agreements.

collective bargaining are numerous and economically relevant. However, let us concentrate on the main elements in bargaining structure and their economic implications.

We might characterise bargaining structure in Britain in the simple way shown in Table 7.1. The left-hand column lists types of agreement, which are largely the same as *levels* of collective bargaining. Almost half of all those covered by a collective agreement are covered by more than one type of agreement. It is not possible from the data to work out the actual combinations of agreements which applied in 1968 but it is clear that many possible permutations exist. Furthermore, the agreement types are listed without reference to the composition of the employer and union sides forming the bargaining unit which produced the agreement – this is significant but it is sufficient for our present purpose simply to identify the levels of bargaining.

Now there are no clear predictions from economic theory as to the economic significance of bargaining structure. However there are some commonsense *a priori* hypotheses which may be advanced. Firstly, we might reasonably suppose that any single settlement level will yield a lower wage outcome than that same settlement level supplemented by another settlement level. For example, we might postulate that industry *plus* workshop bargaining will yield a higher wage outcome than industry bargaining alone. This follows from the assumption that supplementary bargaining is neither neutral nor negative in its effects on wages. Secondly, we might hypothesise that company agreements, in Britain at least, will tend to yield higher wage outcomes than industry settlements. The reasoning behind this hypothesis is that those companies which choose to negotiate outside of industry-wide arrangements do so because there are non-wage benefits for them in it. Consequently, such companies can afford to pay relatively high wages to sustain company bargaining arrangements. For example, in Britain during the late 1960s and early 1970s a number of very large companies such as Shell, ICI, Dunlop and Chrysler opted out of industry-wide bargaining so as to rationalise the structure of wages and the industrial relations system within a company context. Clearly the trade unions would only accept such a move if there were some potential wage inducement to do so. Hence we would expect company agreements to yield higher wage outcomes than any industry-wide agreements.

For the rest, advancing hypotheses is a rather difficult business based at best on intuition and at worst on plain guesswork. So we shall take the issue no further here but return to it with some empirical evidence in chapter 8. Finally, it is worth noting that there is an increasing interest in the relation between bargaining structure and earnings in both Britain and the USA and that a much clearer picture of this relation should emerge over the next few years (see, e.g., Thomson, Mulvey and Farbman, 1977; Kochan and Block, 1975).

Third-party intervention in collective bargaining

In almost all Western industrialised countries collective bargaining is a matter for employers and unions alone. However, in most of these countries there is a process by which third-party intervention may be sought in order to assist the parties to reach a compromise. Third-party intervention normally takes the form of mediation, conciliation, arbitration or some particular process determined by the law of the country in question (such as a labour court).

Conciliation or mediation (they are essentially the same) is the main type of third-party intervention in collective bargaining in Britain and involves a neutral third party assisting the employer and the union to break some deadlock in negotiations. This is usually achieved by the third party bringing new ideas to bear on the issues involved in bargaining, or helping the parties identify more clearly the areas of disagreement and dispelling any distrust or misunderstanding which may be hindering negotiations. The main object of conciliation is to get negotiations moving again on a rational basis.

Arbitration (sometimes through a labour court or other formal tribunal) is also common, but more so in the USA and Western Europe than in Britain. Arbitration is sometimes binding in its effects but sometimes acceptance of arbitration awards is voluntary. Arbitration is quite different from conciliation in that the third party in arbitration is charged to determine a settlement for parties who are unable to agree. This contrasts with the conciliation function which is to encourage the parties to reach an agreement themselves. However, from an economic standpoint, the two processes have something in common.

Third-party intervention is normally sought when one or other party to bargaining expects that the cost of securing an acceptable settlement through intervention is less than that of alternative methods. This sort of situation may arise when one side recognises that it has underestimated the resolve of the other and that the potential costs of obtaining any given settlement are unexpectedly high if bilateral negotiation is pursued. Hence third-party involvement in collective bargaining will generally result from some divergence between the expected and actual progress of collective bargaining, and the party whose expectations are confounded decides that a higher ratio of gains to costs can be secured by third-party intervention (see Hunter, 1977, for a detailed consideration).

Conciliation differs considerably from arbitration in the analysis of bargaining. Conciliation is intended to keep the process of bargaining alive and may be viewed by the party which favours it as a means of modifying the concession curve of the other side. In any event, conciliation does leave the final resolution of an issue in the hands of the bargainers and for this reason may be sought by the party whose expectations are proved inaccurate as a potential additional aspect of bargaining strength which can be discarded if it proves unsatisfactory. No-one has anything much to lose by requesting conciliation since it can be abandoned if it does not produce the results expected of it.

Arbitration, on the other hand, takes the resolution of a dispute out of the hands of the negotiators and is less easy to discard since rejection of arbitration awards devalues the credibility of future arbitration and may actually weaken the side which rejects the award. Hence arbitration may be seen as a process in which concession and resistance curves are discarded and a compromise is left to the arbitrator to find. Arbitration will normally be resorted to where total deadlock between the parties is reached. This is likely to be the culmination of a process in which one party realises that it has misjudged the position of the other and that there is no hope of securing an acceptable settlement (at a reasonable cost) by further negotiation. In addition, experience may have taught either or both sides that arbitration will yield a reasonably predictable outcome. If the expected outcome of arbitration offers a better gain/cost ratio than the expected outcome of continued negotiation, then the relevant party will opt for arbitration.

Hunter (1977) has analysed this process in detail and the interested reader is referred to his work. The general issues involved in third party intervention, as outlined above, are easily incorporated into the Hicks-type bargaining model discussed earlier in this chapter. It is a useful exercise to return to fig. 7.3 and consider how the process of conciliation will modify the relative positions of each side where expectations prove inaccurate and how arbitration abruptly terminates the bargaining process.

A different form of third-party wage fixing exists in most developed countries. This is the machinery which variously fixes minimum or 'fair' wages, etc. In the USA minimum wage legislation affects about six million workers, while wages council orders, etc., in Britain affect around four million workers. These minima are not the outcome of collective bargaining, although unions and employers often have a role in their determination, but are instead a substitute for collective bargaining — usually where the unions are too weak to bargain effectively. The theoretical analysis of wage minima is straightforward: the minimum wage is an imposed supply price for labour, and employers bound to observe such minima simply adjust employment so as to equate the supply price of labour with its marginal product. Where minimum wages are fixed at levels above those that would reflect the work/leisure preferences of the labour force, employment will be less than it would if the labour market were competitive. This is primarily a matter of empirical interest and has been explored as such in various studies.

Summary

In this chapter we have attempted to analyse some economic aspects of the process of collective bargaining. Collective bargaining takes place on a 'contract curve' bounded by economically infeasible combinations of wages and employment. The model on which we have based our analysis indicates the location of the contract curve when demand increases, and therefore provides a basis for identifying the collective bargaining options. A more formal neo-classical approach to this same issue is supplied by the bilateral monopoly model but there are certain assumptions involved in that approach which are unacceptably unrealistic.

Collective bargaining proceeds − in conventional bargaining models − on the basis of bilateral negotiations designed to locate a mutually acceptable compromise settlement. Relative bargaining power determines the course of negotiations and the final outcome. Relative bargaining power is expressed in terms of the strike threat, which in turn is a function of the relative costs to each party of agreeing or disagreeing with the proposals of the other. The realism of this approach is often the subject of criticism from economists and others on the grounds that it assumes an unreasonably high degree of rational calculation by both sides, the availability of large amounts of detailed information to each side about their own and the other's expected behaviour, and the ability to assess probabilities and to discount over time. While one must accept that the conventional bargaining model is not realistic in these respects, there is a case for supposing that both unions and employers learn from experience a sufficient amount about relative bargaining power to make it reasonable to follow the broad lines of the bargaining-model approach as a basis for analysis.

Where both sides calculate and behave rationally and are in possession of all relevant information, strikes will not occur. Where expectations are not fulfilled, information proves inaccurate or either party behaves in an economically irrational way, then a strike may well result.

A limitation of the conventional bargaining model is its assumption that there will always be some fixed amount of utility to be distributed between the two parties. Walton and McKersie have proposed, in the course of a general behavioural analysis of bargaining, that situations exist in which the utility available to be distributed between the two parties may be increased in varying degrees by the actions of the parties to negotiation themselves. The W and M model extends the analysis of bargaining by recognising the existence of a constructive dimension in the bargaining process and by showing that, in general, the contract curve is a more complex concept than is normally admitted in conventional bargaining models.

The structure of collective bargaining may affect the outcome of the bargaining process. This is a hypothesis of fairly recent origin which is currently the subject of some empirical work in Britain and the USA. In the current state of knowledge it is only possible to speculate on how different levels, jurisdictions and compositions of bargaining structure might affect outcomes. Some tentative hypotheses are advanced in the text and some empirical evidence is discussed in the next chapter.

Since third-party intervention in collective bargaining is a feature of the system of bargaining in most countries, a brief account of the economic aspects of arbitration and conciliation is given in the text. In general, conciliation may be viewed as a process by which third parties attempt to modify the concession and resistance curves of the two parties in negotiation, while arbitration cuts short the bilateral bargaining process and imposes a settlement from outside. Minimum wage legislation, wages councils, etc., have the effect of fixing a floor to the supply price of labour and are mainly of empirical interest. Such machinery is usually a substitute for collective bargaining – mainly because unionism is too weak to develop an effective bargaining system – but bargaining often occurs over and above the minima set by the wage-fixing authorities.

We proceed now to consider the empirical aspects of the effects of unions on wages.

Further reading

N. W. Chamberlain and J. W. Kuhn *Collective Bargaining* New York, McGraw-Hill (1965).

A. M. Cartter *Theory of Wages and Employment* Illinois, Irwin (1959).

J. R. Hicks *The Theory of Wages* London, Macmillan (1932).

R. E. Walton and R. B. McKersie *A Behavioural Theory of Labor Negotiations* New York, McGraw-Hill (1965).

G. de Menil *Bargaining: Monopoly Power versus Union Power* Cambridge Mass., MIT Press (1971).

A. Flanders (ed.) *Collective Bargaining* Penguin Books (1969).

CHAPTER 8

Unions and Relative Wages

This chapter is mainly devoted to a review of the empirical evidence on the effect of trade unions on relative wages. Essentially, we are concerned to discover whether or not, and in what degree, trade unions have raised the wages of their members above those paid to similar non-union workers. Hence we are *not* here concerned with the issue of whether unions have caused the *general level of wages* to rise or not (that topic is dealt with in chapter 9). There are some conceptual issues to be dealt with before we proceed to consider the empirical evidence.

The concept of a union relative wage effect

Throughout this book we have so far emphasised that if unions are to provide a positive economic return to their members – which is an important element in the demand for union services – they must do so by raising their members' wages above the rate which their members would receive in the absence of unions. In more practical terms, unions would probably go out of business if they were unable to achieve a positive union/non-union wage differential. Note that the non-union wage is *not* the same as the wage which would prevail in the absence of unions so long as union activity affects non-union wages – which it probably does – but, as we shall see shortly, the only practical measure of union wage effects available is the union/non-union wage differential.

We have already considered the special case of monopsony in the labour market – it is only 'special' in economic analysis; some variant of it is typical of the real world. The first task of a union in a labour market characterised by a positively sloped supply curve of labour is to raise the wage to the competitive level. To do so involves the union in no costs in the form of employment forgone. The net result of a general union wage effect which everywhere and only countered monopsony power would be to establish a perfectly elastic supply of labour at the competitive wage to each monopsonistic employer in the economy. This would yield the same set of wages as a perfectly competitive market would. Empirically we have no way of knowing the degree or extent of union success in countering monopsony, although it would hardly be outrageous to venture the opinion that monopsony-type power has probably been largely eliminated by trade union action.

Unions are most unlikely to be satisfied with merely countering monopsony power, even supposing that they knew at which point they had achieved just that. The whole concept of the union's wage policy being reflected in an internal trade-off between wages and employment suggests that unions are concerned with increasing their members' wages to levels in excess of the competitive rate.

The differential and the state of the labour market

The implication of our assumption that unions will wish to establish a union wage in excess of the competitive rate is that a union/non-union wage differential will result. This differential will comprise both the (positive) wage premium which unions are able to extract from employers and any (negative) depressive effects on the non-union wage which result. We normally measure the differential as the percentage of the non-union wage represented by the union wage premium, i.e. $(W_u - W_n)/W_n$. 100.

Now there is reason to suppose that the union/non-union wage differential will vary according to the state of the labour market. In general, when the labour market is tight we would expect the differential to be relatively small, and when the market is slack we would expect the differential to be relatively large. This follows from the analysis (in chapter 6) of the relative importance of quit and strike threats under different labour market conditions. When the labour market is tight the quit/cost ratio is high relative to the strike/cost ratio and *vice versa* when the market is slack. Empirical evidence strongly supports this hypothesis (see Lewis, 1963a). The importance of this observation is that we must be careful to take account of the state of the labour market at the point in time for which we are estimating the magnitude of the union/non-union wage differential. At certain points in time when the labour market was very tight we might find that the estimated union/non-union differential was either zero or negligible. This does not mean, however, that unions generally have a negligible relative wage effect since estimates made when the labour market is very slack normally indicate a large and significant union/non-union wage differential. See Table 8.3 below for an illustration of this effect.

Unionism and relative wages — some conceptual problems

There are some important conceptual problems in attempting to identify the effects of unions on relative wages. Mostly they relate to situations in which the demand for unionism varies according to the characteristics of workers or those of their employment. For example, it is known that the extent of unionism amongst skilled manual workers is higher than amongst unskilled manual workers. Skilled workers tend both to be more highly paid than unskilled workers and to demand the services of unions more (and be more attractive potential members from the point of view of unions). How are we to untangle cause and effect in such a case? One might argue that the relatively high wages of skilled workers are not caused by a high degree of unionisation but are instead *the cause* of a high degree of unionisation. One might also argue that the two features are simultaneously determined – relatively high wages for skilled workers are *both* a cause and an effect of a high degree of unionism. Again one might argue that high wages are simply a consequence of a high degree of unionisation. All of these are possible hypotheses, and economic theory does not help to discriminate between them.

Similar problems arise with a wide range of worker and employment characteristics. Plant size, industry concentration, sex-mix, educational attainment, labour quality, race, geographical location, training characteristics, propensity to quit and labour turnover are all factors which might be jointly determined by both wages and unionism. Since we cannot sort these matters out on theoretical grounds alone – although the interested reader who wishes to study the many theoretical considerations involved will be enlightened by Johnson (1975), Reder (1965), Levinson (1967) and Ashenfelter and Johnson (1972) – we must bear them in mind in our examination of the empirical work on estimates of effect of unions on relative wages. In general, a failure to take account of the joint determination of wages, unionisation and any of the factors listed above – if they are indeed *economically* jointly determined – will tend to attribute to trade unions a greater effect on relative wages than is the case.

Empirical estimates of the effect of unions on relative wages

Empirical estimates of the union/non-union wage differential are made by regression analysis. There are a great many detailed statistical problems involved in such analysis but it would not be appropriate to deal with these in this book. Lewis (1963a) provides the most detailed and thorough account of the econometric methods involved in estimating union relative wage effects, but his exposition is hard to follow for non-econometricians. A simpler treatment may be found in Metcalf (1977, appendix 2). We shall avoid getting into the complexities of estimating techniques by confining ourselves to some explanatory comments.

The basic equation which is employed in empirical estimates of the union/non-union wage differential is:

$$ln\ W_i = ln\ W_{ni} + \alpha_i \bar{M}; \tag{1}$$

where $ln\ W_i$ is the natural logarithm of the average wage of an industry or occupation i, W_{ni} is the non-union wage in i, α_i is the proportion of the labour force in i who are paid the union wage, and $\bar{M}$ is the average union/non-union differential. In some studies the estimates are made for a sample of individual workers, rather than industry or occupation groups, and in those cases the i's stand for the ith individual and α_i takes a value of 1 if the individual is paid the union rate and 0 if he is not. $\overline{M}$ provides an estimate of the union/non-union differential if we take its antilogarithm and subtract 1. All of this may be taken on faith or explored further by reference to equations (1), (2) and (3) of the appendix to chapter 9, or to Metcalf (1977, appendix 2).

There are two important points to be clear about in the use of this estimating technique. Firstly, the method is really a very simple exploitation of the fact that any weighted average is dependent for its value on its weights. Hence the average wage is treated as a weighted average of the union wage and the non-union wage, the weights being the proportions who are paid the union and the non-union wage respectively. Estimation simply dismembers the average wage into its union and non-union components by applying the appropriate weights to it. Care must be taken to recognise that equation (1) is *not* based on the idea that *union power* is somehow proxied by the inclusion of the proportion unionised in the equation – a trap which many who ought to know better often fall into. Secondly, the non-union wage, W_{ni}, appears as an independent variable in equation (1) but is obviously not directly observable. If we could directly observe the non-union wage all that would be required in order to know the union/non-union differential would be to subtract the non-union wage from the average wage. In estimation, therefore, it is necessary to replace the non-union wage term by a number of variables which we hypothesise will determine the non-union wage. In practice, in the case of a regression across industries, individuals or occupations at a single point in time – a cross-section regression – all that we require is a series of variables which may reasonably be supposed to account for variations in the non-union wage across the sample of industries, individuals or occupations. Care must be taken to ensure that the variables included for this purpose remove as much as possible of the variation in the dependent variable which is due to factors other than unionism. The intention therefore is to end up with an estimate of the union/non-union differential which indicates the difference in the wages of those paid the union rate and those paid the non-union rate by removing all sources of potential differences in wages other than that of union status.

The adjustment vector

The variables chosen to replace the non-union wage in estimation are often called 'the adjustment vector'. It comprises as many variables as economic theory suggests will give rise to variations in wages independent of unionism. Hence we know, for example, that economic theory predicts that the degree of skill possessed by an individual (his 'human capital') affects his wages since his wages include a return to the investments he has made in himself by way of education, training, etc. (the rate of return on investments in human capital). Now if we are estimating equation (1) across a sample of industries we must take account of the fact that there may be differences in the skill composition of the labour forces in each industry and that this will be reflected in differences in the average wages in the sample. In order to avoid attributing wage differences arising from skill compositions to the effects of unions we need to enter a variable in the adjustment vector specifically to take account of inter-industry variations in skill composition. Hence we would normally use a skill-mix variable specified as the proportion of the labour force in each industry who are classed as skilled and the proportion classed as unskilled.

Similarly, in aggregated studies, we would wish to enter a variable which removed variance in the dependent variable due to industry concentration, plant size, sex-mix, labour quality, race or colour, age, experience, education, geographical location, marital status, and so on. All of these factors are capable of giving rise to variations in wages independent of union status, and their influence must be taken account of if accurate estimates of the union/non-union wage differential are to be made. In individual sample studies, additional variables relating to individual characteristics such as health, number of jobs held and so on may be included in the analysis. Since a wider range of such variables are normally available where individual samples can be obtained, the estimate of the differential ought to be more accurate.

Note that a number of variables suggested as appropriate for the adjustment vector have already been cited as potentially determined simultaneously with unionism – where this is the case, the estimated differential will tend to be biased upwards. However, since there is little agreement on the problem of simultaneous determination we must proceed, with caution, on the assumption that these variables are legitimate. We shall in any case soon return briefly to the problem of simultaneous determination in an empirical context.

Estimates of the union/non-union wage differential

The first estimates of the impact of unions on relative wages were made in the USA around 1950. Some were estimates of the union wage effect in individual industries and occupations, and some were economy-wide estimates. During the period 1950–60, over 20 such studies were published and most are reviewed in great detail in Lewis (1963a). Around the middle of the 1960s individual samples became available in the USA owing to changes in the form of the population census, and a number of studies based on this information have subsequently appeared. In Britain the first attempt to estimate the union/non-union differential was made in 1974 but a good deal of work has been done since then. For the rest, there is the occasional study, but very little from outside the USA and Britain.

The US studies published in 1950–60
The various studies reviewed in Lewis (1963a) differ in their methodologies but most are essentially based on a technique similar to that involved in estimating equation (1). Lewis has in fact reworked a number of the studies to standardise

methodology to some extent. It would be tedious simply to repeat his summary of results (Lewis, 1963a, pp. 184—6), so we report only the more interesting cases.

The earliest recorded estimate of a union/non-union wage differential was made for coal-miners in the bituminous coal industry in the USA for the period 1909—13. Greenslade (reported in Lewis, 1963a) estimated that the union/non-union differential in that industry was in the range 38—43%. Greenslade further estimated the differential for subsequent years — up to 1957 — and his estimates show that it was extremely erratic over time, jumping from around 0% to around 40% in a matter of two years. In general, Greenslade's results appear to show that the differential was at its highest when the economy was in deep recession ($M = 120\%$ in 1922 and 57% in 1933) and lowest when the economy was booming ($M = 0$ in 1945). Most of the other industry and occupation studies carried out at this time indicate that the differential was invariably positive although it was normally estimated to be less than the sort of figure estimated for miners by Greenslade. Take two representative years, 1922 as a slump year and 1939 as a boom year, and compare estimates made for different workgroups. Table 8.1 sets out the data and shows that the general order of magnitude of union relative wage effects was under 25% in the inter-war period (although Greenslade's estimates are exceptional) and also that the estimated differential tended to be higher in 1922 than in 1939.

Now the studies cited above do not provide a very good basis for generalisations about the impact of unions on relative wages since they refer to specific employments which will be characterised by special factors — such as differences in the elasticity of demand. Hence a number of attempts were made to estimate economy-wide union/non-union differentials. Again the methodology is similar to estimating equation (1). Table 8.2 gives the estimated differential at various dates. It is not possible to follow the procedure in Table

Table 8.1   Selected estimates of the differential for industries and occupations in the USA

Researcher	Sample studied	Estimated differential (%)	
		1922	*1939*
Greenslade	Bituminous coal-miners	120	30
Sobotka	Unskilled construction labour	–	5
Sobotka	Skilled construction labour	>25	25
Rayack	Production workers in clothing	20	17
Lurie	Motormen in local transport	17	12
Scherer	Hotel workers	–	0

Source: Lewis, 1963a, Table 49, pp. 194—6. All figures are approximate; in each case in which a range is quoted, I have taken a simple average of the high and low figures. All the studies cited are referred to in detail by Lewis.

Table 8.2 Estimates of the differential for the US economy prior to 1960

Researcher	Sample studied	M(%)	Date of estimate
Ross	Manufacturing and mining	10	1945
Ross and Goldner	Manufacturing and utilities	4	1946
Garbarino	Manufacturing	15	1940
Tullock	All workers	<25	1948/52
Tullock	All workers	<30	1953/57

Sources, tc., as for Table 8.1

8.1 and pick out two dates but I have tried to select dates as close as possible to each other.

As may be seen from Table 8.2 we are confronted with a range of estimates which appear to place the union/non-union differential for the USA in the immediate post-war years in the range 4–25%. Lewis himself has set out his own general estimates of the differential for the USA for the period 1920–58 on the basis of the studies cited above and his own work (see Table 8.3). Lewis reports his results in natural logarithms and I have simply computed a percentage effect by taking the antilog − 1. Again, his estimates as presented in Table 8.3 appear to vary inversely with the level of economic activity − we shall return to this shortly. For the rest, the results show that the differential changes quite substantially from period to period and that, with the exception of periods of very high levels of economic activity, unions appear to have had a significant positive effect on relative wages. It should be noted at this stage that some economists have speculated that unions may have had an 'impact effect' on relative wages rather than a continuing effect. The argument is that unions, when they first become established, have a once-and-for-all effect on relative wages but thereafter do not subsequently affect them. (This would be in line with the notion that unions do little more than counter monopsony power.) This is not borne out by a casual glance at the data on the extent of unionism in relation to the estimates in Table 8.3. Unionism fell from about 15% in 1920 to about 9% in 1929 while the differential increased over the period; between 1930

Table 8.3 Lewis's estimates of the union/non-union differential for the USA, 1920–58

Period	Estimated differential (%)	Period	Estimated differential (%)
1920–24	17	1940–44	6
1925–29	26	1945–49	2
1930–34	46	1950–54	12
1935–39	22	1955–58	16

Source: Lewis, 1963a, Table 64, p. 222.

and 1939 unionism increased from about 10% to 19% and, while the differential jumped in the first half of the period, it fell back sharply in the second half, which was the half in which the extent of unionism grew most rapidly; from 1940 to 1958 unionism grew steadily from 20% to 30% and the differential rose, fell and then crept up again during that period. Hence there does not, at this impressionistic level, appear to be much support for the 'impact' hypothesis. Much more appealing is the apparent relation between the differential and the state of the economy.

Since Lewis wrote his book there have been a number of economy-wide studies which tend to estimate a differential for the early 1960s of around 30% (see, e.g., Throop, 1968; Rosen, 1969). However, a major advance in data availability which permitted estimates of the differential to be made on the basis of very large samples of individuals occurred during the 1960s, and estimates based on such samples are thought to be more reliable than those based on aggregates because of the scope provided for constructing a superior adjustment vector. Early estimates using this type of data tended to yield relatively low estimates of the differential. Weiss (1966) estimated a differential for 1960 of 20%, and Stafford (1968) a range of 18–52% for 1966. More reliable estimates have been made by Ashenfelter (1976). He estimates the differential for all workers for 1967 to be 12%; for 1973 to be 16%; and for 1975 to be 18%. These estimates suggest that differentials estimated from aggregate data may contain a significant upward bias, since such estimates for the years covered by Ashenfelter yield higher estimates of the differential.

The spillover problem

In chapter 6 we noted there are likely to be significant spillover effects — that is, wages in the non-union sector of the economy will be influenced by wages in the union sector through such mechanisms as threat effects. Virtually all the US studies of the differential that we have considered above are unable to take account of such spillovers since the data used in estimation identify *union members* rather than *workers paid the union rate*. Although certain of the studies cited use data on collective agreement coverage, these data are unsatisfactory in many of the same respects as straightforward union membership data. In particular, the method of determining 'collective agreement coverage' used by the Bureau of Labour Statistics (BLS) is to count all those employed in an establishment with more than 50% unionisation as 'covered' and all those in establishments with less than 50% unionisation as 'uncovered'. If spillovers are significant this implies that the estimates of the differential which do not take account of them will understate the true differential since they will include in the 'non-union' category some workers who are paid the union wage. Rosen (1969) made an ingenious attempt to overcome this problem in a very complex study which cannot usefully be discussed here. Theoretical methods are, however, unlikely ever to overcome satisfactorily what is essentially a data problem. Fortunately in both the USA and Britain significant advances have been made in recent years as regards the data.

The spillover effect simply means that some non-union workers are paid the union wage. This can arise because of threat effects, by convention, by the criteria of third parties for non-union wage fixing, and so on. The full effect of unions on relative wages can only be identified if the union sector is defined in such a way as to include all or most of the spillover effect. The way in which the data have recently made this definition possible is by enquiry in the standard surveys whether a worker's wage is determined by the terms of a collective agreement or not, rather than whether he is a union member or not. In the USA the union/non-union status information was collected in a supplement to the US Current Population Survey. Since 1975 the survey has enquired whether the worker's wage was covered by a collective bargaining contract or not. If these data include most of the spillover category then they would immediately overcome the problem of spillovers in estimating the differential. However, William Bailey of the BLS is reported by Ashenfelter (1976) to have estimated that the 'union' category formed 90% of the 'covered' category — which implies that spillovers are only 10%. In view of the fact that the 'union' category forms only about 69% of the 'covered' category in Britain, the US data seem somewhat unlikely. There is no way of determining whether the US data understate the extent of the spillover, whether the British data overstate its extent or whether it is really only 10% in the USA and 31% in Britain.

Estimates of the union/non-union differential for Britain

In Britain the first attempt to estimate a union/non-union differential was made by Pencavel (1974), whose estimate refers to 1964. Pencavel used 'union' data and estimated that union workers in industries which did not engage in a significant degree of plant bargaining had a zero differential over non-union workers but that workers in industries which did engage in a significant degree of plant bargaining enjoyed a differential of about 14% over non-union workers. These estimates seemed to indicate that British unions affected relative wages to a significantly lower degree than US unions did. However, after Pencavel's study had been completed, new data on the coverage of collective agreements were published in the *New Earnings Survey* carried out by the Department of Employment for 1973. These data did not simply indicate the extent of union wage coverage but also the extent of coverage of: national agreements only; national plus supplementary agreements; local and company agreements; and no collective agreement. Since these data did appear to capture a significant element of the spillover effect, a number of estimates of the union/non-union differential, as well as the differentials associated with each type of agreement coverage, were quickly made. The studies differ in the samples used and in the components of the adjustment vector; we list the estimates made by each with an indication of differences in sample used but neglect differences in adjustment vectors. The full range of British studies to date is given in Table 8.4.

Table 8.4 reveals a reasonably tight range of estimates of the differential and its components by agreement type with the exception of Stewart's estimate. If we leave Stewart's estimate aside for the moment the differential ranges from

Table 8.4   Estimates of the union/non-union differential for Britain (%)

Researcher	Sample	Date	M	NO	NPLUS	CB
Pencavel (1974)	All manual workers	1964	8	0	14	
Mulvey (1976)	Manufacturing male manual	1973	26	0	41	46
Mulvey and Foster (1976)	All industries male	1973	22	–	–	–
Nickell (1977)	All manual males	1972	18	0	22	20
	All manual females	1972	19	20	9.2	44
Stewart (reported in Metcalf, 1977)	Manual manufacturing manual workers	1971	40		Not known	

*M is the differential for all 'covered' workers over 'uncovered'; NO is the differential of those covered by national agreements only over uncovered workers; NPLUS is the differential of those covered by national plus supplementary agreements over uncovered workers; and CB is the differential of those covered by local and company agreements over uncovered workers.

Dependent variable is gross hourly earnings except in Mulvey and Foster and in Stewart where the dependent variable is gross weekly earnings.

16% to 26% for samples which variously include men, women and manual and non-manual labour. There is, however, some reason to suppose that these estimates may be too high, and further work is being undertaken which ought to clarify this matter. (See Thomson, Mulvey and Farbman, 1977, for some evidence which suggests that the differential may be lower than the estimates in Table 8.4.) Stewart's estimate is based on an adjustment vector which utilises data on personal characteristics taken from the General Household Survey and also employs gross *weekly* earnings as the dependent variable. Certainly this latter feature of his study is known to result in relatively high estimates of the differential (as compared with those made with gross hourly earnings as the dependent variable) and it may be that the personal characteristics data also tend to inflate the estimate.

An interesting feature of the estimates in Table 8.4 is that manual males whose wages are subject only to a national agreement appear to derive no wage premium over the non-union wage. This suggests that national bargaining alone is not sufficiently potent to yield a union wage in excess of the competitive rate or that the 'non-union' wage is determined by reference to national agreements. It is worth reflecting, though, that one quarter of all men in manufacturing industry in Britain are covered by national agreements only and appear to obtain no wage benefit in return. A positive wage premium from collective agreement coverage is confined to the 60% of male manual workers in manufacturing who are covered by national plus supplementary agreements or by company, local, etc., agreements. However, in the case of women this does not apply.

The Pencavel study, as has already been noted, was based on unionisation

rather than wage coverage data and that provides a ready explanation of the
relatively low estimate made. However, Pencavel's estimate refers to 1964 —
something of a boom year — while the other estimates all refer to 1973 — something of a slump year. Hence it may be that his estimate reflects the association
between the differential and the level of economic activity which is evident in
the USA.

Finally, Layard, Metcalf and Nickell (1977) have made estimates of the
differential for Britain on a year-by-year basis between 1961 and 1975. These
are rather *ad hoc* since the coverage variable employed in each year's estimate is
the data for 1973 — the only available series. Hence these estimates require the
assumption that agreement coverage did not vary significantly over the period
1961–75. With that caution in mind the estimates are set out in Table 8.5.

In a regression of the differential on unemployment for the period 1961–75,
it does appear that the differential varies directly with unemployment, which
confirms that the US evidence of this relation is supported on this limited basis
for Britain too.

Some sub-hypotheses concerning the differential
We would expect the union/non-union wage differential to vary according to
certain specific characteristics of different workgroups. Theoretical considerations would suggest:

(a) that skilled workers would obtain a higher differential than unskilled
    workers because the elasticity of demand is lower for skilled than unskilled
    workers (see chapter 5; also Rosen, 1970);
(b) that women would, other things being equal, secure a lower differential than
    men because women are less skilled than men and because unions may
    discriminate against women;

**Table 8.5   Estimates of the union/non-union
differential for Britain, 1961–75**

Year	Estimate (%)	Year	Estimate (%)
1961	18.5	1968	22:1
1962	21.0	1969	23.4 (15.0)
1963	16.2	1970	29.7 (17.3)
1964	17.3	1971	29.7 (18.5)
1965	16.2	1972	36.3 (20.9)
1966	18.5	1973	36.3 (20.9)
1967	18.5	1974	28.4 (20.9)
		1975	36.3 (29.7)

Source: Layard, Metcalf and Nickell, 1977. Figures
         in brackets are based on 1968 SIC class-
         ifications; all other figures are based on 1958
         SIC classifications.

(c) that workers from racial minorities would obtain a lower differential than white workers because they possess less skill on average than white workers and because unions may discriminate against them.

Skill and the differential

In Table 8.6 we report estimates of the differential made for skilled and unskilled men in the USA for 1973. The evidence afforded by Table 8.6 shows that our hypothesis that skilled workers would obtain larger wage differentials than less skilled workers is not supported. In fact the reverse is apparently the case. Possible reasons for this are that skilled workers may lose any special advantage deriving from a low elasticity of demand when they bargain in collaboration with other workers, a practice that is normal in industrial unions and increasingly the case in many other situations, or that unions have deliberately pursued egalitarian policies to advance the cause of the lower paid or, again, that non-union skilled workers are operating in a relatively more favourable market environment than less skilled workers. Moreover, the quit threat of skilled non-union workers is likely to be relatively more potent than that of less skilled workers.

Table 8.6   Estimates of the union/non-union differential for males in construction and manufacturing by skill classes for the USA in 1973 (%)

	Manufacturing[†] USA	Construction USA
Skilled*	7	35
Semi-skilled*	14	52
Unskilled*	21	57

Sources: Data are taken from Ashenfelter, 1976, Table 3.

*These categories are labelled 'craftsmen', 'operatives' and 'labourers' in the US study.

†The data are unweighted averages of durable and non-durable manufacturing estimates.

Women, race and the differential

In Table 8.7 we report estimates of the differential made for men and for women in 1973 for the USA and in 1972 for Britain, and for race in the USA in 1973.

Our hypothesis that blacks would have a lower union/non-union differential than whites is not supported by the US evidence in Table 8.7 — the reverse is evidently the case. Since, as we have already seen, skill apparently confers no positive benefits to union workers — indeed the reverse — the lower average skill of black workers may account for the unexpected high relative differential, and also unions may, in the Equal Opportunities environment, have positively discriminated in favour of blacks. Ashenfelter (1976, Table 2) reports some evidence which suggests that the differential enjoyed by black trade unionists increased from near equality in 1967 with the white differential to its 1973 level and increased again (for men) in 1975.

The hypothesis that women would have a lower differential than men is supported by the US but not by the British evidence. The latter suggests an almost identical differential for both men and women. The British result is hard to explain but may be connected with the growing influence of women in trade unions and also the effects of the Equal Pay Act.

Table 8.7 The union/non-union differential by sex and race for the USA in 1973 and by sex for Britain in 1972 (%)

	Men		Women	
	White	*Black*	*White*	*Black*
USA	17	25	13.5	14
Britain	18		19	

Sources: US data from Ashenfelter, 1976, Table 2, referring to all men and women workers; data for Britain from Nickell, 1977, Table 3, referring to manual workers.

Some further empirical findings
One aspect of union policy which we have already discussed concerns the desire of unions to establish uniform wage rates and conditions throughout their jurisdictions. Unions are generally motivated to pursue this objective in order to protect their most vulnerable members and to restrict the scope for product substitution within the union sector. Empirical studies show that unions have apparently been successful in reducing interpersonal wage differentials (see Lewis, 1963a, for evidence on the USA, and Thomson, Mulvey and Farbman, 1977, for Britain). In general the dispersion of wages within the union sector is

considerably less than in the non-union sector, and on that basis one may infer that unions have reduced interpersonal differentials.

A variety of evidence tends to show that unions have been inclined to reduce geographical, industrial and inter-firm wage differentials, and this is again generally explicable in terms of a desire on their part to protect their weakest members and to limit the potential for competition within the union sector. Little is known about union effects on inter-occupational differentials but it has been argued (Turner, 1957) that the growth of mass unionism with its emphasis on egalitarianism and a policy of flat-rate money wage increases for all has contributed to a narrowing of occupational differentials.

Table 8.8   Union/non-union differentials by components of gross weekly earnings in Britain in 1973.

Component of pay	Union/non-union differential (%)	
	Manual men	*Manual women*
Gross weekly earnings	+ 13.2	+ 19.0
Overtime	+ 37.4	+ 45.6
Incentive pay	+112.7	+ 65.7
Shift premium	+232.4	+400.0
Residual pay	− 0.5	+ 11.1

Source: Thomson, Mulvey and Farbman, 1977, Table 4.

Finally, there is evidence to suggest that unions do not significantly affect union/non-union earnings differentials for hours worked within the standard or basic workweek but instead make all their influence felt regarding overtime rates, shift premiums, bonus pay, and so on. In Table 8.8 the gross weekly earnings of those covered by collective agreements are broken down into their main components and expressed as a set of percentage union/non-union differentials.

Since total hours worked by both the union and non-union workers were similar, the data suggest a union effect which influences the allocation of hours between premium and non-premium rates. Hence the standard workweek for union workers may be shorter than for non-union workers so that a higher proportion of the union workers' hours are paid at overtime rates. However, no complete explanation of these curious and unexpected findings is yet available although a number of possible hypotheses are advanced in Thomson, Mulvey and Farbman (1977). The effects of trade unions on relative wages are evidently not as straightforward as the conventional theory suggests!

Conclusion

There is one crucial matter which we must not lose sight of in considering estimates of union/non-union wage differentials and that is the possibility that wages and unionism are simultaneously determined or that the extent of unionism is determined by the wage. If either of these possibilities were in fact true, then we could not regard estimated union/non-union differentials as an indicator of the magnitude of the effects of unions on relative wages. The conventional view is that estimated union/non-union differentials are indicators of the effects of unions on relative wages, and a number of those who have proposed alternative views have nevertheless continued to publish estimates of the differential on the conventional basis. Ashenfelter and Johnson (1972), Johnson (1975) and Pencavel (1971) have all advanced alternative hypotheses about the relation between unionism and wages but have all been prepared to accept the conventional assumption in empirical work. The existing state of knowledge does not permit us to go further than that. We assume that unions have a unicausal influence on wages, while recognising that this may not be the case and may some time be shown not to be the case.

On that basis we may conclude that unions do influence relative wages and that the magnitude of the union/non-union differential is in the region of 0–40%. Unions affect relative wages to a greater extent when aggregate demand is low (unemployment is high) than when aggregate demand is high (unemployment is low). Unions appear to influence relative wages to a greater extent for less skilled workers than for skilled workers, to a greater extent for blacks than whites in the USA, and to a greater extent for men than women in the USA and about the same for men and women in Britain. The type of agreement coverage also apparently affects the degree to which unions affect relative wages in Britain.

These general conclusions must be tempered by noting that the evidence also suggests that there are wide differences in estimated differentials as between occupations and industries for which we cannot at present account. In view of this, it would be wrong to put too much faith in the precise numerical estimates of the differential presented in this chapter.

Summary

We began this chapter by discussing the way in which a union/non-union wage differential will be established. In general, we would expect increases in union wages to cause a displacement of union labour into the 'non-union sector' of the economy and to depress the non-union wage as a result. Hence the union/non-union wage differential will comprise the union-won wage increase and the union-caused fall in the non-union wage. Unions, however, also affect non-union wages in the opposite way through spillover effects. The main spillover effect is likely to be due to the threat responses of non-union firms who pay wages sufficiently high to prevent a demand for unionisation arising. The net effects of unions on non-union wages depends on the ease of substitution of non-union and union labour, the flexibility of relative wages, and on the extent of spillovers; we shall discuss this in the next chapter.

A simple statistical method of estimating union/non-union differentials exists and depends for its validity on the assumption that unions affect relative wages in a unicausal way. We considered some of the evidence on the effects of unions on relative wages that have been made for the USA and for Britain at various points in time and for various sub-groups. These results and their implications are summarised in the 'Conclusions' section above.

Further reading

H. G. Lewis *Unionism and Relative Wages in the United States* Chicago University Press (1963).
British Journal of Industrial Relations (July 1977, whole issue).
C. Mulvey 'Collective agreements and relative earnings in U.K. manufacturing in 1973' *Economica* (November 1976).
G. E. Johnson 'Economic analysis of trade unions' *American Economic Review* Papers and Proceedings (1975).
O. Ashenfelter 'Union relative wage effects: new evidence and a survey of their implications for wage inflation' Working Paper 89, Industrial Relations Section, Princeton University (1976).

CHAPTER 9

Trade Unions and Wage Inflation

In the last chapter we considered the effects of trade union activity on *relative* wages. In this chapter we consider the effects of trade unions on the money wage *level*. As we pointed out in chapter 8, trade unions may affect the structure of relative wages without affecting the money wage level, so that we are now considering a different dimension of the relationship between union activity and wages.

The general issues

The question of whether or not trade unions cause the general level of money wages to rise is one which has been in dispute almost throughout the post-war period. Before the Second World War steady and prolonged inflation of prices was unknown. During that time prices rose and fell from time to time but did not persistently rise. Wages did rise, however, over the pre-war years but tended to stay in line with productivity changes. For example, in the inter-war years, 1918–39, prices fell by around 23% over the whole period while weekly wage rates rose by about 65%. In the post-war period, however, both prices and money wages rose steadily up until the mid-1960s in most industrialised countries and then accelerated into a very rapid inflation. The wage inflation which occurred during this period exceeded the rate of increase in productivity by a significant amount and was held partly responsible for the price inflation which occurred at the same time. Inevitably trade unions were held by many to be the source of wage inflation.

It would clearly be inappropriate to outline the main elements in the inflation debate in any detail here but a very brief comment is in order (see Trevithick and Mulvey, 1975, for a detailed discussion of inflation). Broadly there have existed two main competing schools of thought about inflation. Up until the mid-1960s these were labelled 'cost-push' and 'demand-pull'. In more recent years the cost-push school of thought is (incorrectly) called 'Keynesian' while the demand-pull school is called 'monetarist'.

The cost-push view of inflation is that autonomous increases in factor costs force prices upwards and that such cost increases have been a major source of upward pressure on the price level throughout the post-war period. Examples of cost-push pressure on prices are 'monopolistic' trade-union-won wage increases, arbitrary rises in some key raw materials prices such as oil, and rising import prices because of devaluations of the currency. Trade unions are usually singled out as the main culprit in the inflationary process since they are the only possible source of persistent cost inflation — dramatic import price rises, etc., tend to occur infrequently — which could possibly explain the persistent price inflation. In any event the cost-push view of inflation regards trade unions as possessing monopolistic power to drive wages up independent of the level of labour demand, and considers that they have used this power and that the consequent increases in money wages have caused price inflation (for a good example of the extreme cost-push view see Wiles, 1973. In the interests of simplicity we ignore intermediate cost-push views.)

The demand-pull school of thought contends that inflation of both prices and wages has been mainly due to the expansive demand management policies of post-war governments implied by their commitment to full employment. On this view the government has persistently run the economy in such a way as to generate an excess demand for labour — i.e. the demand for labour has exceeded the supply of labour at the current real wage — and in consequence the money wage level has persistently risen in order to raise the real wage to its market clearing level. There is controversy over the manner in which the excess demand has been generated — whether it is caused by fiscal or monetary policy — but it is sufficient for us to note that the demand-pull view sees wages being pulled upwards by the pressure of excess demand in the labour market. In the more extreme versions of this hypothesis trade unions have no independent influence on the rate of wage inflation.

The extreme versions of these two schools of thought are in direct contradiction to one another and, since anti-inflationary policy is now the most central element in government economic policy, it is important to try to discover which view is correct. For this reason this chapter is more directly related to vital issues of government economic policy than any other in the book. Let us begin by using the analysis developed earlier to examine the view that trade unions have driven up wages independent of the demand for labour.

Three ways in which unions may cause wage inflation

It is convenient to begin by distinguishing the channels by which unions may cause inflation. There are only three ways in which unions can cause the general level of money wages to rise. Firstly, unions may exploit their bargaining power to push the union wage up so as to increase the union/non-union differential. If the union/non-union differential rises and the non-union wage does not fall to offset this rise, then the result will be a rise in the money wage level. Whether or not this can happen independent of the level of labour demand is a question to which we shall turn shortly. Secondly, unions can recruit non-union workers into their membership, causing a net increase in the proportion of the labour force being paid the union wage, and this will increase the average money wage level so long as the non-union wage does not fall. Thirdly, unions may drive up the union wage and, through a variety of mechanisms, the non-union wage will be induced to rise as a direct result. Let us consider these possibilities more fully. (An elementary mathematical presentation of this proposition is set out in the appendix to this chapter.)

Unions, the differential and the wage level

We have already discussed the means by which unions can drive the union wage up to a level in excess of that which the market alone would establish. In so doing, unions create a positive union/non-union wage differential and we have accepted that the empirical evidence suggests that they have in practice achieved this. Now if the unions force up the union wage so as to increase the union/non-union differential, and the level of aggregate demand at any given price level is not increased, then some union workers are likely to be laid off and increase the supply of labour to the non-union sector, so depressing the non-union wage. Assuming no productivity growth and a fixed total money wage bill, the net effect of this will be to leave the average wage level unchanged, since the fall in the non-union wage will exactly offset the rise in the union wage. However, where some expansion of the total wage bill is possible, it is likely that the fall in the non-union wage will not fully offset the increase in the union wage, and the average wage level will rise. In this way unions can cause inflation, although some might argue that any expansion of the total money wage bill can only occur if governments expand the money supply and thus that it is the *government* which causes inflation.

The above is an account of the impact of union activity on the money wage level on the assumption that non-union markets are competitive. More realistically, we must accept that labour markets are characterised by particularly marked imperfections — many of them a consequence of union-induced relative wage rigidity — and that a swift and complete absorption of the labour displaced as a result of a union-won wage increase into the non-union sector is unlikely to occur. Assuming a simple two-sector economy, much of the displaced union labour will not be qualified in terms of skills and training to move directly into the non-union sector and will remain unemployed in the short run (structural unemployment). In any case, movement between jobs, even where the movers are qualified for existing vacancies, involves job search, which is a costly process involving information-gathering and time-consuming activities, so that some short-run unemployment will exist as people move between jobs (frictional unemployment).

In addition, it may be that the non-union wage is not downwardly flexible owing to social, political, legal and economic factors, so that even when the supply of labour to the non-union sector increases there may be no quick and complete adjustment in the non-union wage to absorb the displaced union labour. Indeed, the displaced union labour may set out with a relatively high reservation wage (minimum acceptable wage) which may make them unwilling to accept jobs in the non-union sector at first, and quite some time may elapse between being displaced and reducing the reservation wage to something close to the non-union one.

To the extent that any of these things occur, the result of the rise in the union wage will be an increased money wage level, as well as increased unemployment in the economy, so long as price rises do not neutralise the wage rises and aggregate money demand does not expand to underwrite them.

The foregoing analysis suggests that a rise in the union/non-union wage differential may cause some increase in the average money wage level and some increase in unemployment. This is due to labour and product market substitution against the unionised sector as a result of the change in the relative wage and price levels of the two sectors. By the same process by which product and labour substitution causes a lowering of demand for the products and labour of the unionised sector in a closed economy, it will cause an increase in the demand for the products and labour of the non-union sector. This will operate partly to counteract the relative wage rise and unemployment in the union sector. The increased demand for the products of the non-union sector will cause the demand for labour in that sector to rise and may cause an increase in the non-union wage. (This gives rise to the concept of an 'optimal union/non-union differential' — see Ashenfelter, Johnson and Pencavel, 1972.) Hence there will be an increase in both the supply and demand for labour in the non-union sector consequent on an initial rise in the union wage and the union/non-union wage differential. However, in the absence of an expansion in aggregate money demand, the net effect of this process will probably still be a net increase in aggregate unemployment.

Union controls on employment

We have assumed that the consequence of an increase in the union wage will be an increase in the supply of labour to the non-union sector, which will depress the non-union wage as a result. This assumption is premised on the notion that unions will respond to a reduction in the demand for their members' services by permitting them to be discharged. It is quite possible, however, that unions will react to the reduced demand for their members' services by worksharing, restricting output or by 'makework'.

Worksharing arrangements are common enough in Britain in recessions and, in the context of the present discussion, could serve to hold union labour in the union sector while product demand switches to the non-union sector and raises non-union wages. Ulman (1955) seems content with this argument and concludes that the union can, by operating worksharing, cause the average wage level to rise. It is difficult to accept that the argument has any real merit. Presumably, worksharing arrangements involve union labour in short-time working, reduced overtime or other practices, all of which have the effect of reducing the hours worked by each individual. Hence, while the average hourly wage rate (exclusive of overtime) may have been increased by the union, the weekly wage and annual income of the union workers may not have risen. We then must dispute which is the relevant index of the general wage level. It is no answer to argue that in the long run the need for worksharing will disappear when aggregate demand rises, because presumably the union will then be prevented from securing a wage increase which it would have obtained in the absence of worksharing. The same arguments apply to restrictions on output, which are the pieceworkers' equivalent of worksharing.

The third category of union responses is called 'makework' by Ulman (1955). Makework restrictions are, according to Ulman, '. . . designed to oblige the employer to hire more labour than he would be otherwise willing to hire at the union wage rate'. This appears to be similar to such things as union-imposed manning levels in Britain. It is difficult to take this argument seriously in so far as it is supposed to relate to the way in which unions might attempt to protect their wage increase and the level of employment over anything but the short run. Makework restrictions cannot be systematically made more and more restrictive to protect each union-won wage increase without rapidly putting employers out of business. Only under draconian assumptions — such as that the industry is wholly unionised, free from any form of domestic or foreign competition and facing a wholly inelastic demand curve — could makework rules be a workable long-run strategy for unions. There is a twist to the argument, however. Ulman maintains that if such devices as worksharing, output restriction and makework prevent an exodus of labour from the union to the non-union sector in the short run, the non-union wage will rise because of the increased demand for the output of the non-union sector, and in that case the differential must narrow as a result. However, as Ulman acknowledges, all of this will in any case increase the price level and, if aggregate money demand does not rise, will lower the demand for all labour and thereby tend to depress both union and non-union wages alike. Further, even if aggregate money demand did rise, no real wage gains for either sector need result from those activities, and we must assume 'money illusion' to make any sense of the whole business.

Substitution of capital for relatively expensive union labour is a long-run constraint on the union's ability to force up wage rates. It could be argued that the phenomenon of makework discussed by Ulman (1955) is more plausibly to be viewed as a shield against this long-run threat to union jobs than as a short-run holding operation designed to insulate the non-union market from unemployment in the union market (see the argument of Weinstein, 1964).

Inflation and the differential over time
Even if we were to accept that union-won wage increases did not depress the non-union wage (and also assume for the moment that they do not increase the non-union wage), the simple proposition that unions can cause inflation by

increasing the union/non-union differential requires that unions *persistently* increase the differential over time. As an empirical matter we know that this does not happen (see chapter 8), so that the argument that union-won wage increases are a causal factor in inflation must depend on a more complex union wage/non-union wage change mechanism than we have so far considered. We return to this matter shortly.

Unions and the natural unemployment rate
It is worth noting at this point that unions may contribute to inflation in another way. Owing to the rigidity in relative wages induced by unions (see chapter 4) and the structural and frictional unemployment which is likely to flow from an increase in the union/non-union wage differential, the process by which the economy adjusts to changes in the structure of labour demand involves quantity or employment changes rather than wage or price changes. In short, union wage activity creates a disequilibrium structure of real wages and employment. Now there is some level of unemployment (which is a proxy for excess demand) at any point in time at which inflation will be steady – this is variously called the 'natural', 'normal' or 'non-inflationary' unemployment rate. To the extent that union wage activity creates structural and frictional unemployment, the natural rate of unemployment will be higher than it would otherwise be. Hence the level of aggregate money demand which is consistent with zero or steady inflation will be lower, the greater the influence of the unions on the structure of real wages (see Flemming, 1976).

Governments, unions and inflation

The foregoing analysis assumes that the level of aggregate money demand is fixed. That device is used to isolate the wage impact of unions from changes in wages which would occur in any case because of increases in the level of aggregate money demand. Consider the reality of government economic policy for most of the post-war period. Inspired by a belief that Keynesian demand management policies had unlocked the secret of a full-employment economic policy, the authorities in the industrial nations of the world committed themselves to pursue full employment as a central objective of policy.

In the knowledge that the authorities would take action to avoid unemployment rising to unacceptable levels, unions could formulate wage policies which attached little weight to the employment costs of rising wages. Hence unions could and did advance fairly ambitious wage claims without overmuch concern as to their employment implications. A rise in the union/non-union wage differential has potential employment costs for unions when the level of aggregate money demand is fixed. When these employment costs manifested themselves in rising unemployment the government, in pursuit of a full employment economy, would typically permit an expansion of aggregate money demand mainly through monetary expansion. The expansion of aggregate money demand validates the union-won increase in wages and union members are either rehired or never laid off. However, the demand expansion is indiscriminate and generates an excess demand for labour in the non-union sector, which in turn causes non-union wages to rise. Hence, in the long run, union and non-union wages rise at about the same rate, the differential remains fairly constant and real wages increase at approximately the same rate as productivity. Now, while unions may be the initiator of the periodic rises in the money wage level which constitute wage inflation, the *government* is the real culprit since it consistently validates each wage rise by monetary expansion and so teaches unions to ignore the possibility of the potential employment costs of their wage policies.

It is only when governments are forced to pursue tight monetary policy that unions begin again to recognise the nature of the trade-off, and the learning process involved is not easy. The British experience since 1974 is a good example of this.

We now turn to the two other channels by which unions may increase the general level of money wages, before we revert to the empirical evidence.

The extent of union wage coverage and wage inflation

It is a simple proposition that an increase in the proportion of the labour force covered by the union wage will increase the average money wage level so long as the union/non-union wage differential is positive. This is simply the result of more people being paid the higher of two wage rates causing the *average* wage rate to increase. This is, of course, a purely mechanical process relating changes in union density to the average wage level but it has been argued that changes in union density are indicative of union 'militancy' (see Hines, 1964). The militancy/union density relation postulated by Hines is based on the idea that unions will conduct recruitment campaigns simultaneously with pressing wage claims on employers. The object of this exercise would be to increase the 'strength' of the union and its capacity to wield an effective strike threat in negotiations with the employer. Serious doubts have been cast on the validity of Hines's approach by Mulvey and Gregory (1977a) and Pencavel (1977). However, there is no way of showing that increases in union density are not related to union militancy although there are more plausible alternative hypotheses. In any case, whatever the source of the change in union density which occurs from time to time, the purely mechanical effect described above will translate such changes into changes in the average money wage level. Trade unions can therefore cause the money wage level to rise by increasing union density although there is a limit of 100% to their ability to do so.

Increases in union density result in an increased proportion of the labour force offering their services to employers at an increased supply price, and all of the analysis which applied to increases in the union wage and the resultant employment effects apply in this instance also at the margin. Hence, to the extent that an increase in union density causes unemployment in the union sector, we would expect increased unemployment in the short run and downward pressure on the non-union wage. This will limit the impact of increases in union density on the general level of money wages. A more important practical consideration which suggests that increases in union density will not be a significant source of pressure on the wage level is the minute changes in union density which have actually occurred in both Britain and the USA. We return to this as an empirical matter later.

Union effects on the non-union wage

We have already recognised that union wage-bargaining activity will affect non-union wages in two possible ways: increases in the union wage may depress the non-union wage through market forces; and increases in the union wage may increase the non-union wage through such 'spillover' mechanisms as the threat effect, convention, legal provision and the attitudes of third parties to non-union wage fixing. We have already discussed threat effects in chapter 6 and, while we accept that they are probably both important and unmeasurable, we noted that the availability of data on union wage *coverage* allows us to go some way towards incorporating them in empirical work. Hence we defer further discussion of threat effects to the empirical work considered later in this chapter. Similarly, wage spillovers from the union to the non-union sector which occur in response to convention or convenience – such as happen where all workers in a partially unionised company, plant or workshop are paid the union rate – have already been discussed and it remains only to treat them empirically in the context of union wage coverage data.

Legislative wage minima

The remaining direct union wage effects on non-union wages fall into two rather similar categories – legal measures and third-party intervention in wage fixing. In many instances these overlap. In almost all of the industrial countries of the world some form of legislation exists to protect vulnerable workers from the worst effects of low pay. In the USA minimum wage legislation affects the wages of millions of workers, in Britain Wages Councils and Fair Wages legislation have the same function. In countries in continental Europe, various legal provisions put a safety net under the lowest-paid workers. Now the importance of these measures from our point of view is that they determine the rate at which the wages of many non-union workers change over time, and this is frequently done by reference to movements in the wages of unionised labour. While it is almost certainly true that legislative measures of the kind mentioned do constitute a spillover from the union to the non-union sector, there are a number of reasons why we should not view the rate of change of the non-union wage as dominated by changes in union wages:

(a) legislation governing changes in non-union wages is frequently based on movements in wage rates (rather than earnings) elsewhere or on price changes;

(b) many non-union workers are not covered by any legislation and, in any case, there is often widespread evasion of legislation by employers;

(c) the wages of workers covered by legislative minima frequently rise more rapidly than the legal provisions alone would account for, and this suggests that market forces have a wage-determining role in these cases;

(d) there is direct evidence that Wages Councils in Britain have at times caused the wage rates which they determine to rise less rapidly than union rates (see *Short Measures for the Poor*, Low Pay Unit, 1977).

However, because legislative provision for wage minima are extremely complex it is simply not possible to determine the extent of spillovers from the union to non-union sectors by this mechanism.

Third-party wage fixing

It is generally held that third parties to wage fixing, e.g. arbitrators, etc., take the prevailing trend in wage movements in general as a benchmark in deciding particular cases. (We ignore third parties charged with implementing legal wage minima since they are covered by the discussion above.) Potentially, therefore, the actions of third parties in wage fixing in the non-union sector are a channel through which spillovers may flow. In practice the vast majority of arbitration concerns the fixing of *union* wages; it only rarely deals with non-union wages.* Further, it is frequently the case that arbitration is sought for some particular dispute, and the outcome must reflect a means of settling the dispute rather than maintaining the wage in question in relation to other wages — although, of course, the 'particular' feature of the dispute may well involve some sort of 'parity' issue. In general, therefore, one might argue that while third-party wage fixing arrangements tend to encourage uniformity in the movement of *union* wages, it is not obvious that they will also serve to link the movement of non-union wages with union wages. Again this is a matter which is best determined empirically.

The influence of union wage changes on non-union changes — some empirical evidence

If movements in union wages have a pervasive influence on the behaviour of non-union wages — through threat effects, conventions, legal provision or

---

*Australia is a special case in this respect due to the fact that arbitration is central to the whole system of wage fixing in that country.

third-party intervention — we would expect:

(a) union and non-union wages to move in close correlation with each other; and, expressed another way,

(b) the union/non-union wage differential to be relatively stable over time.

The facts show that for Britain and the USA neither condition is met.

Consider point (b) first. In the last chapter, Tables 8.3 and 8.5 show the behaviour of the union/non-union differential over time in both the USA and Britain. In the former, where data are available from 1920 onwards, the differential varied from a high of 46% to a low of 2% before 1958 and continued to show marked variation in the period after 1958 (see Flanagan, 1976). In Britain the differential has varied between 16% and 36% in the period 1961—75. Since the union wage is defined as the non-union wage plus the union/non-union differential, variations of this order in the differential imply that union and non-union wages have not changed in close harmony over time.

The test implied by point (a) above is simply a different way of looking at (b). Since no data on the separate behaviour of union and non-union wages over time exist for Britain (except that implied by the time-series of the differential) we must look to US evidence. The most reliable study of this kind is Flanagan (1976). (Flanagan's findings are supported by the other studies of this relation, e.g. Johnson, 1975; Johnson, 1977; Ashenfelter, 1976; and Ashenfelter, Johnson and Pencavel, 1972.) Flanagan finds that the rate of change of non-union wages is not significantly influenced by changes in union wages in a study of US manufacturing covering the period 1959—75. He does find evidence that *union* wage changes are interdependent but concludes that 'Whatever the role of wage contagion among union jurisdictions, the infection apparently has not reached non-union workers by a direct route in recent years' (p. 658).

The conclusions set out above are the only ones that can be inferred from the available empirical evidence. While one cannot be dogmatic about the apparent absence of a close relationship between changes in union and non-union wages on the basis of such evidence, there must be a presumption that no strong relation exists. We must therefore proceed on the basis that non-union wage changes are not in fact largely determined by union wage changes and that it is reasonable instead to assume that non-union wages change chiefly in response to market forces — a conclusion which almost every empirical study supports (see, e.g., Johnson, 1977).

Some empirical evidence on the relation between union activity and wage inflation

So far we have established that:

(a) unions can cause money wage inflation by increasing the union/non-union wage differential under certain circumstances, but that they are also likely to cause unemployment by the same route;

(b) unions can cause the money wage level to rise by increasing union density;
(c) the available evidence suggests that changes in union wages do not determine changes in non-union wages.

Reference to equation (4) in the appendix to this chapter shows that a relatively simple (but crude) method of evaluating the influence of unions on wage inflation exists. At its simplest the method of evaluation involves calculating the change in the union/non-union differential over the time period under consideration; calculating the change in union density which has occurred and estimating how much these factors have contributed to the actual wage inflation which has taken place. The evaluation further involves applying the appropriate coefficients (derived from a simple arithmetic weighting system) to the two effects. This is a technical exercise which may not be easily understood by those who have no mathematical background, so we shall simply note the results of two exercises of this type, one for Britain and one for the USA, and the interested reader is referred to the source publications for the details.

For the USA, Ashenfelter (1976) estimates that the combined effects of the increase in the union/non-union differential and the increase in union density implied a 1.2% union effect on average wages between 1967 and 1973. Total wage inflation over the period was about 44% so that unions contributed an insignificant amount to it. This result is not unique; a similar one is in Throop (1968) and for the whole period 1919–58 a similar finding may be drawn from the work of Lewis (1963a).

For Britain, Mulvey and Gregory (1977b) have estimated that in the period 1961–75 unions contributed about 10% to a total wage inflation of about 170% and that in the period 1967–73 unions contributed a wage rise of 9.9% to a total wage inflation of 70%. The results for Britain have one element of superiority over the US findings in that they are based on *collective agreement coverage* data rather than the straightforward union density data used in the US studies. The advantage of this is that many spillovers from the union to the non-union sector will already be reflected in the coverage data.

Note that these studies implicitly attribute all wage inflation arising from changes in the differential and union density to trade union activity. Market forces and shifts in the structure of the labour force unconnected with union activity could be responsible for these changes, so that the estimates set out above represent the *maximum* effect that unions could have on wage inflation on the basis of our assumptions.

Conclusion

There are a number of ways of analysing the role of trade union activity in relation to wage inflation, and we have chosen a method which logically extends the analysis of unions developed earlier in the book. Other approaches which the reader is urged to consult are to be found in Flemming (1976), Trevithick and Mulvey (1975, ch. 6) and Jackson, Turner and Wilkinson (1972).

The analysis employed in this chapter is not novel and the essential argument which is developed may be traced back to Friedman (1951). The quantitative results tend to confirm Friedman's less detailed findings and are backed up by several studies of the USA — they are not contradicted by any rigorous empirical analysis that this author is aware of. We must therefore conclude that so long as the assumptions on which the evaluation exercise is based are not grossly inaccurate, trade unions in Britain and the USA have had relatively insignificant effects on the rate of wage inflation. Market forces appear, therefore, to have been the dominant cause of wage inflation, and expansionary government policies have probably been the source of the market forces which have caused the rapid wage inflation which has characterised the industrialised countries in most of the post-war period.

Summary

Unions can cause the average money wage level to rise by any of three routes. They may raise the union/non-union wage differential, increase union density or cause the non-union wage to rise more rapidly than it would in the absence of unions.

A rise in the union wage consequent on a rise in the union/non-union wage differential will raise the average money wage level so long as the labour which is displaced from the union sector as a result does not depress the non-union wage to offset fully the union-won wage rise. The exact outcome of a union-won wage rise on the average wage level depends on a number of supply and demand elasticities which cannot be estimated. A union-won wage rise may cause some unemployment and exert some depressive effect on non-union wages. The extent of the unemployment caused and its duration, and the extent of its depressive effect on non-union wages, depends on the state of the labour market, the degree and speed of product substitution against the products of the union sector, the efficiency of job search and the speed of the adjustment process in the non-union sector. We have no reliable information about any of these magnitudes. It is, however, likely that a consequence of a union-won wage increase will be to increase the natural rate of unemployment or — more realistically — the more forcefully unions drive up union wages over time, the higher will be the natural rate of unemployment and the lower the level of demand which is consistent with steady or zero inflation.

Unions may attempt by means of worksharing and makework to avoid the consequences for the non-union wage and member unemployment of an aggressive wage policy. It is difficult to see how these can be effective measures in all but the very short run. It is, however, difficult to discern the actual consequences of a union-won wage increase since governments have, in the post-war period, tended to manipulate the demand level so as to maintain 'full employment', and this involves validating any union-won wage increase at current employment levels. This not only obscures the consequences of union-won wage increases but also casts the government in the role of the culprit in causing wage inflation.

Unions may increase the average wage level by extending the coverage of the union wage by increasing union density. This is a purely mechanical effect and there is no way of knowing whether union militancy and changes in union density are related.

If unions can be shown to cause the non-union wage rise in line with union wages, this would constitute a significant source of union influence on the average wage level. It has often been suggested that unions do cause non-union wages to rise in line with union wages through threat effects, convention, legal provisions for wage minima and by the action of third parties to union wage fixing. There are a number of theoretical and commonsense reasons why this hypothesis should be rejected as a significant phenomenon. Threat effects are limited and tend to stabilise or fall at relatively high levels of unionisation. Conventions by which non-union labour is paid the union rate may be significant but can largely be captured in empirical work. Legal provisions which relate the wages of vulnerable low-paid labour to the union rate are not comprehensive, are evaded and may not in any case employ the union rate as a benchmark in practice. Third parties to wage fixing mainly operate within the union sector and, even where they are concerned with non-union wage fixing, may not apply the union rate as the main criterion. The matter is therefore best resolved by reference to empirical studies. The bulk of the empirical work suggests that there is no close connection between changes in union and non-union wages over time and there is unambiguous evidence that the union/non-union wage differential varies significantly over time. We conclude therefore that union wage activity is not reflected to any significant degree in changes in non-union wages.

A simple method of evaluating the impact of union wage activity on the overall rate of wage inflation for both the USA and Britain suggests that unions have had a negligible impact on the money wage level and therefore, that market forces have determined the rate of wage inflation.

Appendix

The average level of wages may be expressed as an arithmetically weighted mean of the union and non-union wages:

$$W = (1 - \alpha)W_n + \alpha W_u \tag{1}$$

where W, W_n and W_u are the average wage, average non-union wage and average union wage respectively, and α is the proportion of the labour force paid the union wage. Equation (1) is an identity and must always hold true. We may define the union wage as follows:

$$W_u = W_n + \lambda; \quad \text{where} \quad \lambda = (W_u - W_n)/W_n \tag{2}$$

Substituting (2) into (1) gives:

$$W = W_n (1 + \alpha\lambda) \tag{3}$$

Differentiating (3) with respect to time gives:

$$\dot{W} = \dot{W}_n + \lambda/(1 + \alpha\lambda)d\alpha/dt + \alpha/(1 + \alpha\lambda)d\lambda/dt \tag{4}$$

where a dot over a variable indicates a proportional time derivative of the type $dW/dt.1/W$.

It may be readily seen from equation (4) that the three channels by which the union may cause the average wage level to rise are given by the three terms of equation (4), and an evaluation of the impact of unions on wage inflation may be obtained by evaluating each term and its coefficient, although it is normally sufficient to evaluate only the last two terms and treat $\dot{W}_n$ as a residual (see Mulvey and Gregory, 1977b).

Further reading

J. A. Trevithick and C. Mulvey *The Economics of Inflation* London, Martin Robertson (1975).

J. Flemming *Inflation* Oxford University Press (1976).

C. Mulvey and M. Gregory 'The Hines wage inflation model' *Manchester School* (March, 1977).

C. Mulvey and M. Gregory 'Trade unions and inflation in the UK – an exercise' Glasgow University Discussion Paper in Economics no. 22 (1977).

D. Jackson, H. A. Turner and F. Wilkinson *Do Trade Unions Cause Inflation?* Cambridge University Press (1972).

G. E. Johnson 'The determination of wages in the union and non-union sectors' *British Journal of Industrial Relations* (July, 1977).

CHAPTER 10

Unions, Output, Employment and Income

So far we have been mainly concerned with the influence of unions on wages. This is because wages represent the key variable in the union's utility function which it seeks to influence. However, if the wage in any labour market is subject to trade union influence so that it departs from its competitive level, then a number of other variables, including output and employment, will also tend to diverge from the levels which would prevail under competitive conditions. We have already explicitly assumed this to be the case with the employment level by postulating that the union's utility function comprises both wages and employment as arguments. Essentially we are viewing the wage changes as the central element of union policy, and consequential changes in other variables as disutilities which the union must accept as a result of securing any given wage change.

From the point of view of the individual union, its wage policy and its consequences are probably viewed as a simple constrained maximisation problem of relevance only to that union. However, in the wider context of the whole economy we are required to think in terms of the structure of relative wages and the associated structure of employment and output — i.e. the allocation of resources. In this sense we are getting close to non-competitive general equilibrium theory — an area which economic analysis has yet to conquer. All the same, we can reasonably consider some of the issues raised by union influence on wages, and the consequential changes implied for employment and output, without risking a foray into non-competitive general equilibrium analysis. Hence we present some of the analytical issues of interest and also attempt to provide some quantitative evidence.

A related, but distinct, issue which arises regarding the economy-wide aspects of union wage effects is that of the distribution of national income between the factors of production. We shall wish to consider whether trade union activity has the potential for increasing labour's share of national income relative to the shares of other factors (this is *not* related to the distribution of income *within* total wage income) and again suggest some empirical evidence.

Unions and the allocation of resources

The proper framework for this type of analysis is general equilibrium theory but
that theory is difficult and technically advanced, so we shall proceed in an *ad
hoc* way to try to illustrate the main issues involved. (The reader who is
interested in a rigorous treatment is urged to consult Johnson and Mieszkowski,
1970.) We begin by considering how unions might affect employment and
output.

In general, the 'ideal' situation in an economy as regards the allocation of
output and employment will only occur where all markets are perfectly
competitive and all prices (wages) are at their competitive equilibrium levels (for a
given state of technology, income distribution and set of tastes and preferences).
In the technical literature this 'ideal' situation is called a welfare optimum,
though we may (incorrectly but for simplicity) think of it as a situation where
output is maximised within the constraints imposed by the economy's resources.
Since only perfect competition yields an optimum, we can be sure that it
nowhere exists in practice because imperfections exist in almost all markets.
However, since unions specifically set out to raise their members' wages above
competitive levels, they introduce a special set of imperfections into the labour
market and must therefore affect the structure and level of output and
employment.

The firm

In the case of an individual unionised firm the consequences of a rise in the
union wage such that the average wage rises above its competitive level will be a
reduction in employment and output. The rise in the supply price of labour
which results from a union-won wage increase will normally raise the price of
labour relative to the price of capital (assuming for simplicity that only two
factors are employed). In order to maximise profits the employer adjusts to this
situation in two ways: he will substitute relatively cheap capital for relatively
dear labour so that the level of employment will fall (this is analogous to the
'substitution effect' in consumer theory); and he will reduce the level of output
since, even after the substitution effect, the firm's marginal cost will exceed
marginal revenue (this is analogous to the 'income effect' in consumer theory).
Hence the effect of a union-won rise in the wage rate, other things being equal,
will be to cause a reduction in employment (via the substitution effect) and a
reduction in output (via the income effect).

The industry

In the case of a wholly unionised industry operating in a competitive product
market, a rise in the union wage not only causes employment and output to
decrease in the industry as a whole owing to the initial adjustments undertaken

by each individual firm, but also implies an additional fall in output and employment because the product demand schedule for the industry is negatively sloped. Thus the price which accompanies the wage rise causes a lower amount of the product to be demanded and therefore reduces employment and output.

In the case of an industry which is partially unionised the situation is rather more complicated. Assume that the labour concerned is homogeneous, that firms are technically efficient and that the labour market is frictionless. Now an increase in the wages of the union labour (for simplicity 'in the unionised firms') will result in some union labour being displaced and so cause a fall in the non-union wage. Now this may suggest that the decrease in employment and output in the unionised firms would be matched by an equal increase in employment and output in the non-union firms. This is not necessarily so. The effect of the transfer of labour from the union to the non-union firms is to shift men with a relatively high marginal product (the displaced union labour) to the non-union sector, where their marginal product will be lower. Hence total output in the industry may be lower as a result of the union-won wage increase. Employment will also tend to be lower if we drop our assumption that labour markets are frictionless. This situation is shown in fig. 10.1 by reference to the analysis of Rees (1963).

This figure illustrates a partially unionised industry (or, indeed, economy) in which the total supply of (homogeneous) labour is fixed at S. The total demand for labour is given by the line D and the intersection of D with the fixed labour supply schedule S shows us that the competitive wage would be OW_c. Now since the labour force is divided into a union and a non-union sector we will have a

Fig. 10.1

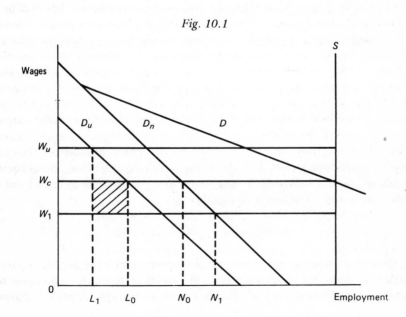

demand curve for union labour D_u, and a demand curve for non-union labour D_u. D_u and D_n sum horizontally to D. Now observe the consequences of the union raising its members' wage from the competitive level to OW_u. At the competitive wage OW_c, OL_0 union workers and ON_0 non-union workers were employed. When the union wage rises to OW_u, the employment of union labour falls to OL_1 and the supply of labour to the non-union sector increases to ON_1. The increased supply of labour to the non-union sector causes the non-union wage to fall from OW_c to OW_n.

Now since the demand curves for both union and non-union labour are marginal product schedules, the area below each curve up to the employment level in each case is the output of each sector. We may measure the output reduction involved in raising the union wage above the competitive wage by measuring the difference between the area under D_u from L_0 to L_1 and the area under D_n from N_0 to N_1. The difference is the shaded rectangle between L_0 and L_1 and this is the output loss due to the union wage rise.

The assumptions on which this illustration is based are restrictive, but relaxing them tends to produce offsetting effects so that the general case is likely to correspond broadly with that illustrated. Ultimately the precise effects on output of a union-won wage increase will depend on the degree to which the non-union sector is competitive, the degree of mobility between the sectors, differences in labour quality and relative demand elasticities (see Rees, 1963).

From the point of view of the economy as a whole in the long run, the distortion of relative wages from their competitive structure due to union activity implies that at any point in time the allocation of labour between its various employments is sub-optimal in a welfare sense. This means that output in the economy is lower than it would be if the competitive structure of wages and employment prevailed.

It should be noted that all market imperfections result in welfare costs to society. Hence product market monopolies which pursue profit-maximising goals will restrict output and employment below their competitive levels, and this will constitute a welfare loss in just the same way as the consequence of trade union activity does.

Some positive effects

Unions are sometimes held to have the effect of *reducing* the level of unemployment below what it would otherwise be, if they are able to increase the efficiency of job search. The argument is that unions supply workers with labour market information more quickly and cheaply than would otherwise be the case and reduce market search time, and therefore frictional unemployment, as a result. Also unions may limit employers' ability to discriminate in hiring and again reduce market search time (see Flemming, 1976).

Another way in which unions are sometimes held to have a beneficial impact on output and employment is via the so-called 'shock effect'. This argument holds that when unions win a wage increase, the employer will respond by innovating capital which improves the efficiency of production. Now there are two cases (at least) here: the employer substitutes labour-saving capital which it would not have been profitable to employ before the union-won wage increase; and the employer is galvanised into introducing capital which would have been profitable to employ even before the union-won wage increase though he did not realise it. The first case is, by definition, impossible. If it *requires* the union to raise wages for the capital to become profitable, then costs and prices must rise, and if the capital is labour-saving, employment must fall. Rees (1962) observes that this argument is frequently cited in rebuttal of the argument that union-won wages increases will cause lower output and employment levels, and disposes of it in the manner that we have. The latter case is inconsistent with the normal assumptions of economic theory concerning efficiency. If it were true in practice that employers were not employing cost-minimising combinations of labour and capital, and union-won wage increases have the effect of making union employers more efficient — such that, say, unit costs did not rise — then unionised firms would never be at a competitive disadvantage relative to non-union firms. This latter proposition is belied by experience in both Britain and the USA (these arguments are due to Rees, 1962).

The magnitude of the cost of the union allocative effect

There have been a number of attempts to quantify union wage effects on employment and output. For the most part these studies have been very crude and their results vary a good deal. The two best-known are those of Lewis (1963b) and Rees (1963). The Lewis study is based on an estimate of the elasticity of relative union/non-union employment with respect to relative union/non-union wages — i.e. the proportion by which an employment transfer from the union to the non-union sector will be of the proportion by which the union/non-union wage differential changes. This elasticity he estimates to be approximately minus unity so that the effect of unions on relative employment will be about the same as their effect on relative wages. Now this implies that a rise of 5 percentage points in the union/non-union wage differential will lead to a fall of employment in the union sector of around 3.8% and a rise in employment in the non-union sector of around 1.3% (assuming that unionisation is initially at about 25%). The change in total employment implied by these figures as the union/non-union differential rises is approximately zero since the non-union sector was much larger than the union sector over the period for which the estimates were made. There are, however, doubts, raised by more recent work and reported in chapter 8, about the accuracy of the estimates of the union/non-union wage differential used by Lewis in his study.

Rees based his study on Lewis's estimates and took account of the output as well as employment effects of union wage activity. Output is judged to be approximately measured by earnings. Using the data for the USA in 1957 Rees estimates a total loss of output approximately equal to 0.14% of the GNP. This estimate is almost certainly too low, for the reasons mentioned in relation to the Lewis study, but even so does appear to indicate that the overall costs to the economy due to the wage-raising effects of unions are very small indeed. This is confirmed by the estimate of Johnson and Mieszkowski (1970) who find that the aggregate welfare cost of union activity is about 0.33%. This conclusion does not necessarily apply to other countries where the union sector is relatively large and where the union/non-union differential may be much larger than in the USA. Unfortunately such studies do not exist for countries outside the USA.

There are, however, some effects of union activity on output which result from non-wage union behaviour and we briefly note these now.

Unions and technical efficiency

Unions may also affect resource allocation by influencing the technical efficiency of the firm. The argument runs thus: employers do not normally actively seek to encourage their employees to unionise and often are prepared to pay the union wage rate to prevent this from happening. The reason why employers wish to avoid unionisation is that unions can effectively protect workers from managerial discipline. Workers wish to have this protection because they can then work less hard, operate more restrictive work practices and are more able to 'get away with' misdemeanours than if they were not unionised.

There is certainly something in this argument. For example, when Esso bought out many of the union-controlled restrictive practices in its Fawley refinery, it is estimated that labour productivity rose by 50% in the following two years (see Flanders, 1964). Moreover Pencavel in a recent study (1977) has estimated that, on the basis of data relating to British coal-mining in 1900–1913, '. . . all other factors the same, a totally unionised coalfield produces some 22% less output than a completely un-unionised coalfield!' He further conjectures that the output of the British economy today is probably even more severely depressed as a consequence of unionism than it was estimated to be in coal-mining at the beginning of the century. Quantitative estimates of this kind are uncommon – owing mainly to the difficulty of making them – and the evidence is chiefly impressionistic. Hence observers have variously accused unions of resisting mechanisation, preventing disciplinary action being taken against workers, condoning absenteeism, defending inefficiency and so on. Perhaps we can end this discussion by quoting the extreme view of Pratt (1904, pp. 25–6) '. . . though there is a universal desire for a fair day's pay (and more, if it can be got), there is an almost universal unwillingness, among those who are subject to trade union influence, to do a fair day's work'.

Unions and the distribution of income

In the previous sections of this chapter we have been concerned with the effects of unions on the allocation of resources. We now turn to the related question of unions and the share of national income accruing to labour.

In the simple neo-classical model the national income is distributed between the factors of production – labour, capital, land and enterprise – according to the marginal product of each factor and the proportions of each factor employed in the productive process. At its simplest the competitive neo-classical model predicts that each of the factors of production will receive as its price the value of its marginal product, so that the share of any factor in national income will simply be the product of its marginal product and the units of the factor employed. Now trade unions may be introduced into this analysis as the only market imperfection without in any way changing the above general proposition and without altering the share of national income going to labour. This is so because we do not normally assume that trade union wage-raising activity also raises the marginal product of labour as a whole or affects the total amount of labour employed. This is because rises in the marginal product of union labour resulting from union-won wage increases will be matched by falls in the marginal product of non-union labour if all labour markets are frictionless. Hence the immediate prediction from the simple neo-classical model is that unions will not alter the functional distribution of income as between the factors of production.

We have, of course, already seen that owing to imperfections in the adjustment process in labour markets, in practice union wage-raising activity is likely to lead to falls in employment and output. There is no ready way of moving from this observation to a prediction about union influence on income distribution. We cannot know whether the employment and output effects of union activity affect the employment and marginal product of the other factors proportionately or differentially. For example, if the union raises the union wage and an (imperfect) market adjustment process occurs whereby union employers substitute capital for labour and non-union employers substitute labour for capital, we have no *a priori* way of knowing whether the capital/labour ratio as a whole has changed and, consequently, no way of knowing whether capital and labour share the income loss equally or unequally. The simplest production functions predict equal sharing and, therefore, no change in the distribution of income.

Ultimately theories of the functional distribution of income depend for their predictions about relative income shares on the assumptions made about the degree of homogeneity of the production function, the elasticity of factor substitution and the nature of technical progress. No set of such assumptions is demonstrably superior to any other and the very simplest model – a Cobb-Douglas production function and neutral technical progress – fits the observed facts quite well. However, it is certainly true that there are assumptions under which unions can increase labour's share of national income. Robinson and

Eatwell (1973), for example, have argued that unions can bring about short-run changes in labour share of national income. By introducing substantial market imperfections into the analysis, short-run adjustment to changes in relative prices will be slow and sometimes incomplete, and this will permit unions to influence labour's share in the short run. However, in the long run it remains the case that there is no compelling reason to suppose that unions can or do influence labour's share of national income.

The observed facts of the functional distribution of income over time show a fair degree of stability in relative factor shares after adjusting for employment changes. This is true of almost all the industrialised countries in the world and in some cases has been true for over a century. Apart from cyclical changes in income distribution — which may be accounted for more easily than not by factors other than union activity — the long run is characterised by fairly stable factor shares as predicted by the simple neo-classical models, although labour's share has increased somewhat in Britain and the USA over the last century.

Some empirical evidence

Various pieces of empirical evidence have suggested that union-won wage increases have increased labour's share of national income from time to time (Phelps Brown, 1957; Glyn and Sutcliffe, 1972; Robinson and Eatwell, 1973). However, these studies have been based on fairly casual theories of income distribution and demonstrate only that short-run changes in factor shares may have been connected with trade union activity and that long-run changes in factor shares are mainly due to structural and secular trends. The only really sophisticated study of this phenomenon is by Johnson and Mieszkowski (1970), and their conclusion is that union activity has had no significant effects on the functional distribution of income and that the gains of union labour are made at the expense of non-union labour, not profits.

We are forced to conclude, therefore, that unions probably have no appreciable influence on the long-run distribution of factor incomes although, because of imperfect adjustment, they may influence income distribution in the short run. This is entirely what we would expect on the basis of conventional theory as well as the historical evidence that factor shares have tended to be remarkably stable over long periods of time.

Summary

In this chapter we have briefly reviewed the argument that unions have imposed welfare costs on the economy by bringing about a misallocation of resources as a result of their influence on the level and structure of wages. Further, we examined the case for supposing that unions may have influenced the functional distribution of income.

If unions raise the union wage above its competitive level, then employment and output in the union sector will fall as employers substitute capital for labour and unit costs rise. If labour markets were frictionless, then adjustments would occur so as to reduce the non-union wage and maintain the *total* employment level, though some loss of output would nevertheless be experienced. Under less restrictive assumptions however, it is likely that both output and employment would fall since labour markets normally display marked imperfections. However, empirical estimates of the output and welfare losses resulting from trade union wage effects appear to indicate that these losses will be negligible. Another way in which unions may affect the level of output is through direct restrictions which take the form of union work rules and a variety of other activities which shield union labour from direct management control. Little is known of the magnitude of these effects but tentative estimates show that they may be potentially very significant.

We also considered whether unions might influence the functional distribution of income. Our conclusion was that this is unlikely to be the case in the long run, although short-run changes in income distribution may well result from union activity because of imperfect market adjustment processes. There are assumptions which may be built into income distribution models which do permit union wage activity to cause a rise in labour's share, but there is no theoretical reason to suppose that these assumptions are valid. The empirical observation that factor shares have remained fairly constant over long periods of time in a large number of countries seems to suggest that unions have not influenced factor shares.

Further reading

H. G. Lewis 'Relative employment effects of unionism' *Industrial Relations Research Association Proceedings* (1963).

H. G. Johnson and P. Mieszkowski 'The effects of unionisation on the distribution of income: a general equilibrium approach' *Quarterly Journal of Economics* (1970).

A. Rees 'The effects of unions on resource allocation' *Journal of Law and Economics* (1963).

J. H. Pencavel 'The distributional and efficiency effects of trade unions in Britain' *British Journal of Industrial Relations* (July 1977).

J. Robinson and J. Eatwell *An Introduction to Modern Economics* New York, McGraw-Hill (1973).

CHAPTER 11

Economic Policy and Unions

This chapter departs somewhat from the tone and method of the rest of the book. So far I have presented a sketch of the economic theory which provides a framework for the analysis of trade union activity, and have reported empirical results which assist in quantifying aspects of that theory. Here I turn to the question of whether or not, and what, implications for economic policy appear to emerge from the foregoing analysis. This is clearly a normative task and my own views are therefore based on personal judgments.

Do unions create economic problems?

Policies are usually formulated to deal with problems. Hence, if we are to consider economic policies in relation to the activities of unions we must first establish that unions are the source of economic problems. The empirical evidence suggests that unions have apparently had a rather limited impact on the sort of economic variables which give rise to concern on the part of the authorities. While unions do appear to have had a significant effect on the relative wage structure, this has not, it seems, been reflected in any significant welfare costs to the community. Similarly, unions have not evidently been a major source of inflationary pressure as compared with market variables and the monetary policy of governments. Nor, it seems, have unions distorted the functional distribution of income in any significant way, so that they have probably not, in this way at least, acted as an important constraint on the rate of growth of the economy. Hence in these matters it appears that unions, despite their apparent stature in the economic affairs of the industrialised economies, are fairly innocuous institutions.

In general, therefore, policy issues raised in relation to trade unions tend to revolve around industrial relations matters such as the legality of picketing, the status of the closed shop, the legal immunity of trade unions, industrial democracy, social-security payments to strikers' families and so on (see Whigam, 1961). These issues are peripheral to the subject matter of this book and are therefore not discussed further. One economic issue which has attracted a lot of attention in recent years, however, is prices and incomes policy.

142

Prices and incomes policy

In chapter 9 we found little reason to suppose that trade unions directly cause inflation. Hence incomes policies designed to reduce the rate of increase of wages by voluntary or statutory restraint on trade unions cannot be successful in curbing inflation. Since inflation is essentially a process determined by the forces of monetary demand, only monetary restraint can curb it. However, as inflation is moderated by a policy of monetary restraint, the union-induced inflexibilities in the structure of relative wages throw the burden of adjustment on to employment rather than wages. Hence, when a policy of monetary restraint is employed to curb inflation and wages continue to rise, unemployment will inevitably rise also. Unions can make no lasting *real* wage gains for their members since price rises neutralise wage rises. Unions are therefore faced with a choice between wage restraint and relatively low unemployment or an unrestrained rise in money wages and relatively high unemployment.

Since governments generally wish to avoid high unemployment they adopt incomes policies. However, the real choice ought to lie with the unions. Unions cannot really wish to see money wages race ahead with no lasting real gains to their members while unemployment rises inexorably as a result. It is in the interests of the unions to moderate the rate of increase in money wages so that their members are no worse off in real wage terms but are better off owing to unemployment being lower than it otherwise would be. Incomes policies or wage restraint policies are, accordingly, in the interests of the unions, although they must be designed to avoid distortions of the wage structure, and unions should not therefore need to be persuaded to accept them by government.

When we talk of unions in this context we talk of unions as a whole. It is true that some unions may make relative real gains for their members at the expense of the members of other unions and at the expense of non-union labour in the course of an unrestrained wage inflation. It is perhaps this consideration that motivates certain unions to resist incomes policies.

Unions and governments

One of the great difficulties encountered in the matter of unions and government policy — as generations of legislators have found — is to determine the 'legitimate' scope for union activity. Only totalitarian governments deny trade unions the basic right to organise and to engage in collective bargaining. However, in the democracies it has proved difficult to decide whether the state should adopt a neutral or biased stance towards trade unions. The great variety of legislation concerning the rights of unions in industrial relations matters in different countries indicates the extent of this dilemma. In some countries, Britain in the last few years in particular, the government has adopted a pro-union stance (see Pencavel, 1977). This is most obvious in the very extensive rights and immunities which unions enjoy within the law to extend their organisation, establish closed shops and engage in picketing and secondary boycotts. (In Britain most of these rights now derive from the Trade Unions and Labour Relations Act of 1974.) In other countries, e.g. the USA, governments have adopted a distinctly more neutral stance towards unions and have limited their rights within the law to a far greater extent than in Britain.

Unions are unique institutions within society so that there is no way of arguing that they should be treated within the law 'just like everyone else'. Since this criterion is unavailable, the legislative climate within which unions operate is normally determined by the political persuasion of the government. Hence any judgment about whether unions are treated 'too favourably' or not in legislation will be a reflection of the degree to which the political persuasion of the observer differs from that of the government. It is in this light that the discussion below should be viewed.

Throughout this book we have analysed union activity on the assumption that *some* measure of competition in labour markets exists. If competitive behaviour is absent from labour markets, the tools of conventional economic analysis become largely incapable of explaining labour market behaviour in much the same way as they would be redundant in attempting to analyse the labour market in, say, the Soviet Union. It is not the overt intention of any of the governments of the Western democracies to bring about a situation in which trade union organisation is so extensive as totally to eliminate competition in labour markets. In such a situation the wage level and wage structure would be determined by union fiat and the labour market would be constrained to function by a system of non-price rationing which could have potentially disastrous consequences for the economy.

Britain is undoubtedly approaching this sort of situation more quickly than any other Western economy. The Trade Union and Labour Relations Act of 1974 and the Employment Protection Act of 1975 are the sources of pressure in this direction. In keeping with the general focus of this book we shall not concern ourselves with industrial relations issues, such as closed shops, picketing, etc., and instead confine ourselves to two more clearly economic issues albeit with strong political overtones. The issues discussed are explicitly raised by Pencavel (1977) as 'undesirable' features of state policy in the British labour market, and it is approximately that judgment of them on which the discussion below is based.

The political influence of unions

It is hardly controversial to assert that the trade union movement in Britain has, in the post-war years, exerted considerable influence on the policies pursued by both Labour and Conservative governments. For the most part Conservative governments have recognised in the trade union movement a powerful adversary and have at various times accommodated the unions on a number of issues but more generally have been concerned to avoid conflict with them. In contrast, Labour governments have effectively been drawn into a political alliance with the unions and have positively promoted policies designed to further the political aspirations of the unions. It would be hard to explain the promotion of the Trade Union and Labour Relations Act of 1974 in any other way. While in certain other countries – notably in Scandinavia – close links between socialist governments and the unions exist, they have not, as yet, solidified into the type of alliance which has existed in Britain in the last few years.

Let us say then that the unions have a substantial input into the political and economic policies which governments of any persuasion will follow. What then is the substance of this input? Unions aspire to be champions of the 'working class' – not only their own members – against the alleged abuses of the capitalist system. In Britain the Labour party owes its origins to the political initiatives of the trade union movement, and the unions see themselves as the industrial wing of a broad labour movement of which the Labour party is the political wing. The alliance has not always been a happy one but increasingly has become an effective one. None of this is exceptional unless it provides a channel of influence to the trade unions through which they are enabled to exert an economic influence well beyond that which they are capable of doing through the industrial activities we have analysed in this book.

Let us try to identify the more important issues of this kind and offer some general suggestions for economic policy.

Unions, the state and economic policy

It is in practice difficult, if not impossible, to distinguish between those policies which government has introduced specifically to satisfy the aspirations of the trade union movement and those which happen to suit the interests of the trade union movement but which are introduced for other reasons. Much of social policy falls into this category. However, the following policies are so closely in line with the aspirations of the trade union movement that their influence in policy formulation must, directly or indirectly, have been very significant (see Pencavel, 1977).

The nationalisation of industry

Unions are most effective in gaining their wage objectives where they are dealing with state monopolies which are largely free from the discipline of competition and where, as successive governments have demonstrated, the state will provide an apparently inexhaustible supply of finance to avoid the collapse of the industry or, more recently, even any significant adverse economic consequences for the labour force. In such situations the unions are largely freed from the constraint of the employment costs normally associated with an aggressive wage policy. British Steel, British Shipbuilders and Rolls-Royce are examples of monopolies which have recently been taken into state ownership, in large part at the behest of the trade unions. All persistently make losses yet all are amongst the highest wage firms in the country with active and aggressive trade union policies being pursued with little fear of resultant job losses.

The older vintage of nationalised industries vary in their economic circumstances but invariably pay relatively high wages and have militant trade unions within them. (I exclude the Post Office from this group for various reasons.) Unions operating in this environment are not, in any real sense, engaged in an economic struggle with 'capital' nor are they operating against the background of the usual rules of the market; instead they are often thought to be engaged in extracting from the public purse as much as they can in the knowledge that redundancies (lay-offs) are a remote prospect and that losses consequent on their activities will be made good by way of subsidies or political price policies which consumers are more or less obliged to accept (see Phelps Brown, 1973).

Unions are amongst the leading advocates of the nationalisation of industry in Britain and, on the view advanced above, it is not hard to see why (see Ostergaard, 1954). Those who pay the price for the economic gains made by the unions in these industries are held to be consumers, the economically inactive and the taxpayer. Moreover, since many of the industries concerned persistently lose money for reasons connected with their lack of commercial viability − over and above any union-induced problem − they constitute a source of resource misallocation which imposes costs on the whole community. None of this is to be understood as an argument against the principle of state ownership of industry − it is instead an argument against the nationalisation of industry in the interests primarily of placating the desire of unions for a favourable environment in which to pursue their sectional objectives at the expense of the remainder of the community.

A policy suggestion
The answer to any problems of this kind which exist does not lie in the denationalisation of state-owned industry. Instead the following general approaches which might have the effect of restoring some of the constraints on trade union activity which the private sector must face, would be more appropriate. Firstly, the nationalised industries could be given *firm* commercial objectives to pursue and permitted a significant degree of autonomy in pursuing them. Secondly, and following from the first, the nationalised industries could be given the authority freely to negotiate with unions and to make labour redundant where this is a commercial corollary of the wage outcomes of collective bargaining. Freedom in this sense would mean freedom to raise prices or to lay off surplus labour where this is commercially desirable or designed to meet clearly defined criteria of utility maximisation. Thirdly, where appropriate, competition in the nationalised industries could be encouraged. To a limited

extent this has been done in the case of the airlines and steel but is apparently not to be permitted in other cases such as shipbuilding.

These are not dramatic statements. They are intended to suggest ways of limiting the potential political power of the unions, the response of government and the consequent economic power which the unions may have to extract more and more from the consumer and the public purse without paying heed to the economic and social implications of their activities (see Pencavel, 1977, for another approach).

Unions, unemployment compensation and statutory wage minima

Unions cause unemployment to be higher than it need be when they cause the real union wage to be above its 'full employment level' and encourage government to set rates of unemployment compensation at relatively high levels. We have already argued that unions can set the real wage at a level higher than the marginal product of the labour force, and in addition cause frictional and structural unemployment to exist by distorting the structure of relative wages. Now unions can only sustain such a situation so long as they are able to limit competition from the unemployed, the non-union labour force and the potential for product substitution against the union sector. Competition in both the labour and product markets is often restricted by certain devices which have the force of law and which have been promoted by governments in response to trade union pressure. (Among these is the closed shop but we shall neglect that issue here.) Firstly, competition for jobs from the unemployed may be restricted in the short run (and it is the short run which is important here) by the high level of unemployment compensation; this is a consequence of the system of earnings-related unemployment benefits introduced in 1966, which resulted in a jump in the ratio of average short-term unemployment compensation to post-tax average earnings from 49.3% in 1965 to 73.2% in 1967 and a current figure in the region of 75%,* and the fact that unemployment compensation is index linked to prices. The effect of this high relative level of unemployment compensation must be to raise the reservation wage of redundant workers and greatly to increase the average market search time of the unemployed (see Maki and Spindler, 1975). The resource cost to the economy of this factor is probably significant and one of its main effects is to permit the employed union labour force to enjoy real wage levels in excess of labour's full employment marginal product. Again, it is argued that it is the taxpayer, the consumer and the economically inactive who finance the excessive real wages of employed union labour.

Secondly, for a very long time institutions designed to prevent non-union wages from approximating to their competitive levels have existed and have been

---

*In 1969 the figure was 71.0% in Britain as against 51.4% in France and 37.1% in Germany (see Flemming, 1976, pp. 50—1).

actively encouraged and promoted by the unions. Agricultural Wage Boards, Wages Councils, Fair Wages Resolutions and, more recently, Schedule 11 of the Employment Protection Act of 1975, all have as their purpose, *inter alia*, the maintenance of non-union wages in excess of their competitive levels. Much of the support for these measures does of course come from a sense of philanthropism and social justice. An economic effect of these measures, however, is to restrict effective wage competition for union labour in employments where unions find it difficult or impossible to regulate wages through conventional methods. The consequences are an artificially protected high relative real wage for union members and an unnecessarily low level of employment of non-union labour. Relatively high union wages are on this view financed by the unemployed, the taxpayer and the consumer.

These measures impose costs on many sectors of the community and are often based on confusion and ambivalence. Almost all of the statutory wage provisions are based on the notion that there exists, independent of economic criteria, some 'fair wage'. There is no such thing as a 'fair wage'. Whatever wage is determined by the interaction of the marginal product of labour and the supply price of labour is 'fair'. The idea of a 'fair wage' is normally confused with the idea of a socially acceptable income — a quite different concept. Most people would not resist the notion that our society has a duty to ensure that individuals and families are not forced to live in poverty through no fault of their own. To try to achieve this objective by distorting relative wages is partially to defeat the objective in the process and to bring about distortions in the allocation of resources.

So far as the high relative level of unemployment is concerned, the problem is largely one of resource misallocation bought by the community at a high price. It is difficult to see how any society can justify a system of unemployment compensation that encourages people to prefer unemployment to work and to pay to the unemployed more than a substantial proportion of the workforce can earn in work. Quite apart from the perceived 'unfairness' of such a system it has the effect of reducing the inflation threshold of aggregate demand and probably has serious consequences for the growth potential of the economy. Nor is it likely to be an efficient way of achieving its ostensible social objective of shielding the unemployed from poverty. An economic rationale for the system that has occasionally been advanced is that it permits workers who are laid off to engage in efficient search activity. There is no evidence that this has been the case and, indeed, any theoretical arguments in support of this idea are weak to say the least (see Tobin, 1972; and *D.E. Gazette*, October 1976, p. 1096).

The ambivalence which is associated with high unemployment compensation ratios relates to the continual demands emanating from the trade unions for the government to adopt policies which will decrease the unemployment level, while at the same time advocating the continuance of the unemployment compensation ratios which are in part to blame for the high level of unemployment in the first place and which then act as a rigid constraint on the government's ability to act without serious economic consequences to reduce unemployment.

A policy suggestion

Curiously there exists a ready-made policy which would apparently fulfil the main social objectives of both the unemployment compensation system and the problem of low pay, without bringing about any serious resource costs. The objective of the system must be to ensure that all individuals and families should be protected against poverty whether in or out of work. Such a system could be operated on the principle of a negative income tax or a tax credits scheme which was indexed to the average earnings level, accompanied by the abolition of statutory wage-fixing machinery. This would ensure that the low-paid were not also low income groups in the same proportion and would, incidentally, tend to reduce the supply of hours of work to low-paying employers and consequently force up the competitive wage. It would also ensure that the social objectives of protecting the unemployed from poverty were provided for without making many of them prefer unemployment to work. What it would *not* in general do is ensure continued protection for the unionised labour force from competition from the unemployed and the low-paid.

Conclusion

We have identified in this chapter two areas in which trade unions may have been able to promote their own interests through their power to influence government. They may have achieved this at substantial cost to the community as a whole. The measures in question – nationalisation of industry, high unemployment compensation ratios and statutory wage minima – have not been exclusively promoted by trade unions since they are espoused by other groups as means of achieving various social and political objectives. It is, however, undeniable that the trade union movement in Britain, and to a lesser extent in some continental European countries, has been able to exert effective pressure on government and, in the case of the policies we have discussed here, has been amongst their leading advocates. Indeed, as Pencavel (1977) has pointed out, much of current trade union thinking on political and economic matters is confused and contrary to the traditions of trade unionism. Phelps Brown (1973) has observed:

> If the whole of the dividends and interest paid out by British companies in 1971 had been sequestrated and applied to raise pay without any provision for the maintenance of those who lost retirement incomes or trust and insurance funds, average earnings would have been raised by less than 14%; and this would have been once and for all. The outcome is that collective bargaining today is not between labour and capital, or employees and management, for the distribution of the products of particular industries between pay and profit; but between different groups of employees, for the distribution of the national product between them one with another, and between them as a whole and the inactive population.

If trade unions wish to pursue the type of struggle identified by Phelps Brown, there is no particular reason why government should wish to stop them. However, neither government nor the community should be prepared to permit the unions progressively to alter the rules of the game if in pursuit of their objectives they encroach on the overall welfare of the whole community as a result.

Further reading

J. H. Pencavel 'The distributional and efficiency effects of trade unions in Britain' *British Journal of Industrial Relations* (July 1977).

E. H. Phelps Brown 'New wine in old bottles: reflections on the changed working of collective bargaining in Great Britain' *British Journal of Industrial Relations* (1973).

J. Flemming, *Inflation* Oxford University Press (1976).

M. Friedman 'Some comments on the significance of labor unions for economic policy' in D. McC. Wright (ed.) *The Impact of the Union* New York, Harcourt Brace (1951).

R. E. Hall 'The rigidity of wages and the persistence of unemployment' *Brookings Papers on Economic Activity* 2 (1975).

M. L. Wachter 'Some problems in wage stabilization' *American Economic Review* Papers and Proceedings (1976).

E. Whigam *What's Wrong with the Unions?* Penguin Books (1961).

G. N. Ostergaard 'Labour and the development of the public corporation' *Manchester School* (1954).

Bibliography

J. Addison and J. Burton (1977) 'The institutionalist analysis of wage inflation: a critical appraisal' *Research in Labor Economics* vol. 2.

O. Ashenfelter (1976) 'Union relative wage effects: new evidence and a survey of their implications for wage inflation' Working Paper 89, Industrial Relations Section, Princeton University (August).

O. Ashenfelter and G. E. Johnson (1972) 'Unionism, relative wages and labor quality in U.S. manufacturing industries' *International Economic Review* (October).

O. Ashenfelter, G. E. Johnson and J. H. Pencavel (1972) 'Trade unions and the rate of change of money wages in U.S. manufacturing industry' *Review of Economic Studies* (January).

O. C. Ashenfelter and J. H. Pencavel (1969) 'American trade union growth: 1900–1960' *Quarterly Journal of Economics* (August).

G. S. Bain and F. Elsheikh (1976) *Union Growth and the Business Cycle* Oxford, Blackwell.

J. Barbash (1956) *The Practice of Unionism* New York, Harper & Row.

J. L. Baxter (1973) 'Inflation in the context of relative deprivation and social justice' *Scottish Journal of Political Economy*.

G. S. Becker (1959) 'Union restrictions on entry' in *The Public Stake in Union Power* Charlottesville, University of Virginia Press.

K. E. Boulding (1963) *Conflict and Defence* New York, Harper & Row.

A. Briggs (1964) 'The social background' in Flanders and Clegg (1964).

A. M. Cartter (1959) *Theory of Wages and Employment*, Illinois, Irwin.

N. W. Chamberlain (1951) *Collective Bargaining* New York, McGraw-Hill.

N. W. Chamberlain (1961) 'Determinants of collective bargaining structure' in A. R. Weber (ed.) *The Structure of Collective Bargaining* New York, Free Press of Glencoe.

N. W. Chamberlain and J. W. Kuhn (1965) *Collective Bargaining* New York, McGraw-Hill.

G. Cyriax and R. Oakeshott (1960) *The Bargainers* London, Faber.

H. B. Davis (1941) 'The theory of union growth' *Quarterly Journal of Economics* (August).

G. de Menil (1971) *Bargaining: Monopoly Power versus Union Power* Cambridge Mass., M.I.T. Press.

M. Dobb (1929) 'A sceptical view of the theory of wages' *Economic Journal*.

P. B. Doeringer and M. J. Piore (1971) *Internal Labor Markets and Manpower Analysis* Lexington, D. C. Heath.

Donovan Commission (1968) *Report of the Royal Commission on Trade Unions and Employers Associations* London, HMSO (Cmnd. 3623).

J. T. Dunlop (1950) *Wage Determination under Trade Unions* New York, Kelley.

J. T. Dunlop (1957) 'The wage structure: job clusters and wage contours' in G. W. Taylor (ed.) *New Concepts in Wage Determination* New York, McGraw-Hill.

R. J. Flanagan (1976) 'Wage interdependence in unionised labor markets' *Brookings Papers on Economic Activity* 3.

A. Flanders (1964) *The Fawley Productivity Agreements* London, Faber.

A. Flanders (1969) (ed.) *Collective Bargaining* Penguin Books.

A. Flanders and H. Clegg (1964) (eds.) *The System of Industrial Relations in Great Britain* Oxford, Blackwell.

B. Fleisher (1970) *Labor Economics: Theory and Evidence* Englewood Cliffs, Prentice Hall.

J. Flemming (1976) *Inflation* Oxford University Press.

M. Friedman (1951) 'Some comments on the significance of labor unions for economic policy' in D. McC. Wright (ed.) *The Impact of the Union* New York, Harcourt Brace.

A. Glyn and B. Sutcliffe (1972) *British Capitalism, Workers and the Profits Squeeze*, Penguin Books.

R. J. Gordon (1976) 'Recent developments in the theory of inflation and unemployment' *Journal of Monetary Economics* (April).

R. E. Hall (1975) 'The rigidity of wages and the persistence of unemployment' *Brookings Papers on Economic Activity* 2.

J. J. Healy (1965) (ed.) *Creative Collective Bargaining* Englewood Cliffs, N.J., Prentice Hall.

J. R. Hicks (1932) *The Theory of Wages* London, Macmillan.

A. G. Hines (1964) 'Trade unions and wage inflation in the United Kingdom: 1893−1961' *Review of Economic Studies* (October).

C. C. Holt (1971) 'Job search, Phillips' wage relation, and union influence: theory and evidence' in E. S. Phelps (ed.) *Microeconomic Foundations of Employment and Inflation Theory* London, Macmillan.

L. C. Hunter (1977) 'Economic issues in conciliation and arbitration' *British Journal of Industrial Relations* (July).

R. Hyman (1973) *Strikes* London, Collins.

D. Jackson, H. A. Turner and F. Wilkinson (1972) *Do Trade Unions Cause Inflation?* Cambridge University Press.

G. E. Johnson (1975) 'Economic analysis of trade unions' *American Economic Review, Papers and Proceedings*.

G. E. Johnson (1977) 'The determination of wages in the union and non-union sectors' *British Journal of Industrial Relations* (July).

H. G. Johnson and P. Mieszkowski (1970) 'The effects of unionisation on the distribution of income: a general equilibrium approach' *Quarterly Journal of Economics*.

J. Johnson and M. C. Timbrell (1974) 'Empirical tests of a bargaining theory of wage rate determination' in D. E. W. Laidler and D. L. Purdy (eds.) *Inflation and Labour Markets* Manchester University Press.

J. M. Keynes (1936) *The General Theory of Employment, Interest and Money* London, Macmillan.

T. A. Kochan and R. N. Block (1975) 'An interindustry analysis of bargaining outcomes: preliminary evidence from 2-digit industries' Cornell University (June) mimeograph.

R. Layard, D. Metcalf and S. Nickell (1977) 'The effect of collective bargaining on wages' paper presented to the International Economic Association Conference on Personal Income Distribution, Noordwijk-aan-Zee, Netherlands (18−23 April).

H. M. Levinson (1967) Unionism, concentration and wage changes: towards a unified theory' *Industrial and Labor Relations Review*.

H. G. Lewis (1963a) *Unionism and Relative Wages in the United States* Chicago University Press.

H. G. Lewis (1963b) 'Relative employment effects of unionism' *Industrial Relations Research Association Proceedings*.

B. J. McCormick and E. O. Smith (1968) (eds.) *The Labour Market* Penguin Books.

R. B. McKersie and M. Brown (1963) 'Non-professional hospital workers and a union organizing drive' *Quarterly Journal of Economics* (August).

D. R. Maki and Z. A. Spindler (1975) 'The effect of unemployment compensation on the rate of unemployment in Great Britain' *Oxford Economic Papers*.

A. Marshall (1920) *Principles of Economics* 8th edn, London, Macmillan.

D. Metcalf (1977) 'Unions, incomes policy and relative wages in Britain' *British Journal of Industrial Relations* (July).

C. Mulvey (1968) 'Unemployment and the incidence of strikes in the Republic of Ireland' *Journal of Economic Studies* (July).

C. Mulvey and J. A. Trevithick (1974) 'Some evidence on the wage leadership hypothesis' *Scottish Journal of Political Economy*.

C. Mulvey (1976) 'Collective agreements and relative earnings in U.K. manufacturing in 1973' *Economica* (November).

C. Mulvey and J. I. Foster (1976) 'Occupational earnings in the U.K. and the effects of collective agreements' *Manchester School* (September).

C. Mulvey and M. Gregory (1977a) 'The Hines wage inflation model' *Manchester School* (March).

C. Mulvey and M. Gregory (1977b) 'Trade unions and inflation in the U.K. – an exercise' Glasgow University Discussion Paper in Economics, no. 22.

S. J. Nickell (1977) 'Trade unions and the position of women in the industrial wage structure' *British Journal of Industrial Relations* (July).

G. N. Ostergaard (1954) 'Labour and the development of the public corporation' *Manchester School*.

J. H. Pencavel (1970) 'An investigation into industrial strike activity in Britain' *Economica*.

J. H. Pencavel (1971) 'The demand for union services: an exercise' *Industrial and Labor Relations Review*.

J. H. Pencavel (1974) 'Relative wages and trade unions in the United Kingdom' *Economica*.

J. H. Pencavel (1977) 'The distributional and efficiency effects of trade unions in Britain' *British Journal of Industrial Relations* (July).

S. Perlman (1928) *The Theory of the Labor Movement* New York, Kelley (reissued 1949).

E. H. Phelps Brown (1957) 'The long term movement of real wages' in J. T. Dunlop (ed.) *The Theory of Wage Determination* London, Macmillan.

E. H. Phelps Brown (1973) 'New wine in old bottles: reflections on the changed working of collective bargaining in Great Britain' *British Journal of Industrial Relations*.

E. A. Pratt (1904) *Trade Unionism in British Industry* cited in Pencavel (1977).

R. Price and G. S. Bain (1976) 'Union growth revisited: 1948–1974' *British Journal of Industrial Relations*.

D. L. Purdy and G. Zis (1974) 'On the concept and measurement of union militancy' in D. E. W. Laidler and D. L. Purdy (eds.) *Inflation and Labour Markets* Manchester University Press.

M. W. Reder (1952) 'The theory of union wage policy' *Review of Economics and Statistics*.

M. W. Reder (1959) 'Job scarcity and the nature of union power' *Industrial and Labor Relations Review*.

M. W. Reder (1965) 'Unions and wages: the problems of measurement' *Journal of Political Economy*.

A. Rees (1951) 'Postwar wage determination in the basic steel industry' *American Economic Review*.

A. Rees (1952) 'Industrial conflict and business fluctuations' *Journal of Political Economy*.

A. Rees (1962) *The Economics of Trade Unions* University of Chicago Press.

A. Rees (1963) 'The effects of unions on resource allocation' *Journal of Law and Economics*.

L. G. Reynolds (1964) *Labor Economics and Labor Relations* Englewood Cliffs, N.J., Prentice Hall.

B. C. Roberts (1962) *Trade Unions in a Free Society* London, Hutchinson.

D. H. Robertson (1931) 'Wage grumbles' in *Economic Fragments* London, King.

D. H. Robertson (1957) *Lectures on Economic Principles* London, Collins.

J. Robinson (1934) *The Economics of Imperfect Competition* London, Macmillan.

J. Robinson and J. Eatwell (1973) *An Introduction to Modern Economics*, New York, McGraw-Hill.

S. Rosen (1969) 'Trade union power, threat effects and the extent of organisation' *Review of Economic Studies*.

S. Rosen (1970) 'Unionism and the occupational wage structure in the United States' *International Economic Review*.

A. M. Ross (1948) *Trade Union Wage Policy* Berkeley, University of California Press.

S. Rottenberg (1953) 'Wage effects in the theory of the labour movement' *Journal of Political Economy*.

F. P. Stafford (1968) 'Concentration and labor earnings: comment' *American Economic Review*.

G. W. Taylor (1957) (ed.) *New Concepts in Wage Determination* New York, McGraw-Hill.

A. W. J. Thomson, C. Mulvey and M. Farbman (1977) 'Bargaining structure and relative earnings in Great Britain' *British Journal of Industrial Relations* (July).

A. Throop (1968) 'The union-nonunion wage differential and cost-push inflation' *American Economic Review*.

J. Tobin (1972) 'Inflation and unemployment' *American Economic Review*.

J. A. Trevithick (1976) 'Inflation, the natural unemployment rate and the theory of economic policy' *Scottish Journal of Political Economy* (February).

J. A. Trevithick and C. Mulvey (1975) *The Economics of Inflation* London, Martin Robertson.

H. A. Turner (1952) 'Trade unions, differentials and the levelling of wages' *Manchester School*.

H. A. Turner (1955) 'Trade union organisation' *Political Quarterly*.

H. A. Turner (1957) 'Inflation and wage differentials in Great Britain' in J. T. Dunlop (ed.) *The Theory of Wage Determination* London, Macmillan.

H. A. Turner (1962) *Trade Union Growth, Structure and Policy* London, Allen and Unwin.

L. Ulman (1955) 'Marshall and Friedman on union strength' *Review of Economics and Statistics*.

M. L. Wachter (1976) 'Some problems in wage stabilization' *American Economic Review* Papers and Proceedings.

R. E. Walton and R. B. McKersie (1965) *A Behavioural Theory of Labor Negotiations* New York, McGraw-Hill.

A. R. Weber (1961) (ed.) *The Structure of Collective Bargaining* New York, Free Press of Glencoe.

P. A. Weinstein (1964) 'The featherbedding problem' *American Economic Review*.

L. W. Weiss (1966) 'Concentration and labor earnings', *American Economic Review*.

E. Whigam (1961) *What's Wrong with the Unions?* Penguin Books.

P. Wiles (1973) 'Cost inflation and the state of economic theory' *Economic Journal*.

D. McC. Wright (1951) (ed.) *The Impact of the Union* New York, Harcourt Brace.

W. Zeuthen (1930) *Problems of Monopoly* London, Routledge.

Author Index

Subject Index